# Earth Speaks

## Messages from Mother Earth

*Pamela Kribbe*

BookLocker

Saint Petersburg, Florida

Print ISBN: 978-1-64719-260-0
Epub ISBN: 978-1-64719-261-7
Mobi ISBN: 978-1-64719-262-4

Published by BookLocker.com, Inc., St. Petersburg, Florida.

Printed on acid-free paper.

BookLocker.com, Inc.
2021

First Edition

Translation by Maria Baes and Frank Tehan

# Contents

# Introduction

We know our planet, the earth, as the palpable background of our daily life. The earth is present in the ground beneath our feet, in the nature that surrounds us, in the body we inhabit. It is present in our food and drink, in the rhythm of day and night, in the wind that touches our skin. But who or what is the earth anyway? Is it just a massive rock that carries us, a dead lump of matter floating aimlessly through the universe? Or is the earth an animate creature with its own voice and face?

This book posits that the earth is an inspired and conscious being, with whom you can connect and communicate on a subtle level. Human consciousness is not the only form of consciousness. Animals also have awareness, although this is different in nature than human consciousness. More and more animal studies show that animals can experience sophisticated emotions. According to research, plants seem to react to the way people approach them. Careful, loving treatment seems to stimulate their growth and flowering. This indicates that plants have a consciousness that can record people's thoughts and feelings. Even stones have a degree of consciousness. It is possible to feel the energy of gemstones working on you; they can have a powerful, healing effect.

What about the earth itself? The earth is a planet, which at first glance seems nothing more than a massive chunk of rock moving through space. Thanks to the Sun and the atmosphere, it is possible, from a chemical viewpoint, that life exists here. This is what science tells us. The question then arises. Is the earth just a lump of matter, or is it the consciousness that inhabits, animates, and gives life to this matter? You may ask the same question about yourself. Are you your body or are you the consciousness that bears and animates your body?

These questions are vast and all-encompassing and the subject of centuries of philosophical discussion. In this book, the assumption is that everything that lives is animated by a "something" that is independent and precedes the material form in which it resides. The earth is not primarily a material chunk of rock; the earth is a conscious and intelligent being. It is possible to communicate with the soul of the earth. This book aims to give the earth a voice and to allow it to speak. Here you will find a series of messages *from* the earth.

I now write Earth with a capital letter so that the word becomes a proper name: the name of a unique, living being. The messages from Earth are about Earth itself, about we humans, and about the relationship between humans and Earth. Earth would like to make contact with us so as to remind us of an old agreement, an old covenant that exists between it and we humans. It is in the loving cooperation of humans and Earth that we both find our destiny, that we both experience joy and fulfillment.

## What is channeling?

How does my communication with Earth take place? How did I receive the messages and how do I know if they are reliable?

The messages in this book have been received by way of channeling. During the process of channeling – literally *channeling* – you, as a human being, are open to the energy and wisdom of a spiritual presence that is not in an earthly body. You feel connected to an energy stream that transcends you and gives you a loving message that is enlightening and encouraging. During a channeling you will receive insights and inspiration, which you verbalize or write down in words.

When you channel, you find yourself in a state of spiritual relaxation, which is comparable to the sense of flow that you can have when you are inspired by something; for example, creating music, doing a sport or painting. You are outside of your mind and deep in your bodily feeling. As a channeler, you are also actively present in this open and receiving state because you form the bridge between the intuitively felt insights and their representation in human language. The channeler is the interpreter who translates the intuitively received and felt insights into words and concepts.

Channeling is an engaging source of information, which can shed new light on different themes and bring you into contact with the widest and deepest dimension of your soul, the larger dimension of Being behind the physical. Channeling can lift you out of your earthly worries, connect you with a broader perspective and thus give you hope and insight. Nevertheless, channeling is, and remains, a human activity that, like other human pursuits, varies in quality and originality. Relying on a spiritual entity as a source of your message does not suddenly make the information in that message more valuable. The criterion of whether the information is valuable or not is always something you must judge with your common sense and intuition. If the information is enriching, stimulating, enlightening, and inspiring, then it is good and you may be helped by it in your daily life. If the message is judgmental, frightening, biased, or very dramatic in tone, then there is reason to seriously doubt its value.

The question that channeling often raises is: how do you know if you are a clear channel; if you receive the messages pure and unfiltered? You can assume that every message is filtered through the human mind and the social culture in which you are raised. It is not as if you can totally turn yourself off as the recipient of a message. In my view, channeling is a collaboration between the person and God, between the human world and the spiritual world, in which a person is present as an active, conscious co-player. I do not think the art of pure channeling requires that you turn yourself off so you are a passive medium, but that in communicating with the spiritual world, you give the best of your gifts and talents.

The best thing you have to give is your trust, openness, and courage. These qualities make you surrender, as unbiased as possible, to the flow of spiritual energy that seeks to manifest itself through you. In receiving that flow, you will work with your mind and intellect to best share the energy and insights that you feel in human language. Words, concepts, and language belong to earthly reality. The contact with the spiritual world is often very direct and emotional. We need a human translator who gives this energy an earthly form. In this translation, some distortions can and will occur. Purity does not stand or fall with perfection, but with sincerity and a sense of one's own limitations.

As a reader of a channeled message, you can never know exactly what is distorted and what is not. If the channeler is pure, he or she usually does not know either, because the distortion takes place unconsciously. That is why it is so important to judge a channeled message on its content. Feel from your own intuition and common sense whether or not it is valuable to you.

From a modern perspective, it is a strange idea that Earth has a living consciousness that you can communicate with. Both science and dualistic traditions of spirituality reject this possibility. Before I tell you how contact with Earth began for me, I would first like to let Earth itself talk about the possibility of contact between humans and Earth:

*Communicating with the living nature around you is a very natural thing and can help you feel more at home on the Earth. What you call supernatural or paranormal is actually very natural and normal. Look around you in nature. Intuitive perception is quite normal for animals. In contact with their young and their own kind, animals often communicate telepathically, not in words and concepts. Animals can feel earthquakes and tidal waves coming before the technology designed by humans has registered anything. Plants can also perceive intuitively, they can sense moods and react to them, although they do not know the emotions of humans and animals.*

*In nature as a whole, there is a flow of communication that is based on the inner connection between all living beings. In all nature, the hand of God is at work, not as a defining or commanding hand, but as a gentle, living stream of spirit that manifests itself in a thousand and one forms and remains the One in everything.*

*In humans, this natural flow is disturbed by the presence of an overactive intellect. Thinking, which is analytical and ordering in its nature, has value and usefulness. However, thinking has become the smothering overgrowth in humans and has removed them from their own naturalness. Essentially, it is natural and normal to intuitively communicate with the living beings around you. People today find it strange to talk to animals and plants. They have convinced themselves that they are the only conscious beings on Earth. The animals and plants by their very nature feel absorbed in an animated whole; humans have disowned themselves from this natural whole. They feel like an errant loner in a cold and meaningless universe.*

*In this book, I call on you to return to nature, especially to your own nature, your feelings, your heart, that which makes you part of the whole. It is possible to do so, simple even. All you have to do is to move along with the music of your heart. It is about listening to the language of your own nature again, and not rejecting it out of fear or because of learned intellectual considerations. I call you to a new wildness. Not a wildness that disturbs harmony, but one that restores harmony and brings you home to your indestructible, divine core, which cannot be understood or tamed by the human mind.*

For me, feeling a living contact with Earth has certainly not been a matter of course. I began receiving channeled messages from Earth in 2007, when I had been involved with my practice for years and had already published several books with channelings, mostly inspired by the Christ's energy. It was not natural for me to focus on the Earth. By this I mean that, partly unconsciously, I had many prejudices and reservations about my being on Earth in a physical body. In me lived old beliefs that the body is a dungeon for the soul, that the Earth is a valley of tears, and that, above all, spirituality helps you transcend the earthly. So, I myself was full of dualistic ideas, which I felt came from both the spiritual tradition in which we all grew up and from previous life experiences that were not positive and which had caused in me a resistance to being incarnated on the Earth.

The inner contact with Earth has taught me to gradually let go of these ideas. Feeling her wisdom, originality, and strength was, and still is, a wonderful experience. Earth has a highly developed, sparkling consciousness; she has depth, humor, and realism. In speaking with her, the image of a young woman in a light-colored dress sometimes appears, fresh as Spring, dancing in the wind. In her transparent eyes I see images of nature light up: ancient rocks, jagged tree roots, tender flowers, the eyes of a tiger, a deer disappearing behind the trees. Images that help me to experience the presence of the soul of the Earth in a most tangible way. She *is* the living nature around us, and she is more than that, she is that which animates all forms of life on the Earth, and she gives us the opportunity to explore and experience life here in this dimension.

In the messages I have received from Earth, her call to connect is heard again and again. Earth wants to tell us a different story about our destiny as human beings than what has been told to us by the dualistic traditions of the past. Our earthly nature, including our emotions and passions, is not sinful, low, or suspect. The intention is not to transcend the earthly within ourselves and to reach out to a higher reality beyond the Earth. Instead, when we turn to the earthly and natrural within ourselves, and listen to it and work with it, we come home to ourselves and to the Earth. The path is not about transcending the earthly, but more pointedly about the art of embodying your soul and descending with it into the earthly reality *here* and *now*. On this path of descent, the soul of the Earth wants to receive and empower us.

"Heaven on Earth" is not a distant dream, Earth stresses. Every human being is capable of creating a piece of paradise on the Earth, first and foremost by living in harmony with themselves. In this book, Earth invites you to come home to yourself. If you can work with nature within you, it will automatically lead to you honoring the nature around you and engaging with it from a place of connectedness.

All the messages in this book have emerged from channelings received in the presence of a group of interested people, on the occasion of a lecture or workshop. The messages were edited and supplemented by me afterwards, always adapting to the flow of energy and information I felt coming to me from Earth. During the workshops and lectures, I was always accompanied by my partner Gerrit Gielen, and his presence has been essential for the creation of this book.

## Human beings and Earth

I am the voice of Earth, and I salute you in joy. I am pleased about the connection we are making. You are my child, yet at the same time, you are my parent. I am your mother, yet you act as my steward and caretaker of the Earth. You have been born from my womb and I enabled your soul to take form in a physical body. Your form was shaped by my hands, as does a potter shape clay, and in my hands you are still cherished. It is my continuing desire to protect and nurture you with my love and encouragement.

Feel my presence in and throughout your body. We are not separate – I communicate with you through your body. Let me help you to now relax, to let go of all the tension in your head, your neck and shoulders. A warm shower of gentle Earth energy now releases you of all the thinking and worrying you humans are so used to doing. I am here to tell you that you are fine just as you are. My energy feels warm and familiar to you, and with a spark of humor. Allow my energy to flow though your heart, your abdomen, your legs and feet, and connect you with the ground beneath you. Recognize your kinship with me – *we are one*.

The great secret of life on Earth is that all beings that live here are of one essence. The minerals, the plants, the animals, and the humans are connected by a web of consciousness that encompasses all beings. All nature is silently aware of this connection; it is only humans who seem to have forgotten. Although surrounded by a multitude of life forms – all conscious at some level – humans still feel lonely and lost in the universe. And this is tragic, though not without meaning or purpose. Humanity has embarked on an adventure, and forgetting was part of that adventure. Sweet human child, you have not made a mistake, in the ordinary sense of the word. You plunged into a great adventure when once you departed Home.

Home is not a place. Home is a primal sense of safety; a natural Beingness with no questioning of yourself and worrying about where you are going and what it is all for. *Home is a state of consciousness,* a sense of your own spirit so that you feel safe and free, a sense of peace and tranquility. Home is neither up in heaven, nor does it reside in the past or in the future – *Home is in your heart*. You left Home the moment you forgot you are one with everything around you. You lost the self-evident sense of connectedness, which all beings of nature possess unconsciously, when you started to believe you were separate from everything and that you were independent and autonomous. It was then that you started to experience fear and loneliness.

## The adventure of creation

The experience of forgetfulness and getting lost shows both your great strength *and* your great vulnerability. The very possibility of disconnecting yourself from the all-pervading oneness, and deeming yourself independent from the web of life, shows you have a strongly focused consciousness that is a creative force. Your consciousness was so strong and dynamic that it wanted to transcend the boundaries of what is self-evident. And in order to discover and experience what is self-evident – as it actually is – you first have to disconnect from it. You probably know the saying: "You don't know what you got until it's gone". You had to forget the truth before you could truly and consciously know it. You had to leave Home in order to recreate it within your own hearts. Your consciousness had to turn itself inside-out in order to eventually understand what and who you are. This turning inside-out created the illusion of separation and fear, and, by doing that, it lead you to a wrong image of reality – but it also showed your great creative power.

I do not have that kind of creative power; I do not create as you do. I will give you an example to illustrate this difference. When a human holds a flower in its hand and really admires it, something happens to the flower. If you had etheric eyes, you would see a flow of light going from you to the flower, and when that light is taken in by all her cells; the flower will gain in life force and beam her loveliness even more. Humans can give life force to plants and flowers by their appreciation and admiration. The flower receives this energy as spiritual food that reinforces the flower's self-awareness and makes it even more lovely and vibrant. In this way, humans can inspire nature and help it gain in self-awareness.

My, or nature's, power is not to create, but to receive; I receive energies and pass them on. I receive energies from the cosmos, from the Sun and the planets, and from the realm of humanity, and I transform these energies so they can take form in an earthly way. *I am a great transformer of energies!* I receive and then I give back, but I do not create as do you humans. I am like the flower who gathers in your light and beams it back to you. I, and all my realms of nature, admire your creative power. Through your creative consciousness, I am able to grow in awareness. And as you lose track of what you are, I can remind you, and thereby become more conscious myself.

At this stage of your journey, you feel homeless and lonely, although you are starting to again long for unity and connectedness. This longing leads to growth in consciousness among humans and the realms of nature benefit from this – *they grow with you*. They are becoming more consciously aware of themselves. As you become more conscious of the unity and connectedness between all that lives, you become the stewards and teachers of the natural realms on Earth. As I told you, I am your mother, but I am also your child. I want to learn from you and to share in your experiences so that I myself acquire experience and raise my awareness.

Do not feel shame because you are a human; being a human is something grand. Humans are the great "forgetters", but also the creators of new paths in consciousness. You are masters at opening up unexplored territory – you are pioneers. Humans have received the gift of free will so they are able to disconnect from the whole and steer their own course. They can create new realities based on their desires, dreams, and intentions. This freedom has been granted to you because in the heart of the cosmos there is faith in humanity.

There is much fear, anger, and resistance in humans. In the past, humanity has explored the extremes of pain, destruction, and suffering. Yet deep within the cosmos there is still faith in humanity, faith in *you*. Being human can lead you to become entangled in persistent illusions of fear and desire for power, yet there is also a great promise in the heart of humanity. The moment humans remember the oneness and connectedness of all being, they themselves become divine, loving beings who elevate life around them and inspire it to grow in self-consciousness and self-realization. Human beings have a type of consciousness that can give a powerful evolutionary impulse to all living beings on Earth.

## The promise of cooperation

I, Earth, and the realms of mineral, plant, and animal; of air, fire, water, and earth, are waiting for you – we wait for your awakening. When you awaken, your collective consciousness will lift us to a new level of consciousness. We do not wait passively – *we reach out to you*. We can help you to remember who you are by reminding you that you are safely held by Powers that transcend the human state and that have your best interests at heart.

*We long to embrace you!* Be receptive to nature and feel that you are allowed to ease back into the unconditional safety of Being itself. You need not fret and stress so much about getting your life together – let *life* take care of that. There is a rhythm and wisdom inherent in nature that is communicated to you through your body and your feelings. You are used to thinking too much and then basing your actions *on* your thinking, but the flow of feeling inside you often points in another direction. Feeling comes from within and thinking often comes from without, and it is this difference that causes so much conflict between what you feel deeply within and what you think you ought to do or be in the outside world. I encourage you to trust your feelings more and to let the voice of your heart speak openly.

In practice, you can do this by giving more attention to the signals your body sends to you. Your body is an extraordinarily rich instrument; it is not a mere shell, a material fabric in which your soul is wrapped. Your soul manifests itself in and through your body, and speaks to you through your body much more directly than through your thoughts. Make it a habit to frequently ask your body how it is feeling: "Is there tension or pain somewhere?" And then direct your attention to those areas. Ask for the emotion behind the bodily sensation to show itself to you, but do not make doing this difficult. Do not think: "What emotion could possibly be hiding here?" *Feel what is there!* If you do not feel anything, let it go for awhile – the answer will come to you.

Wait patiently and know that the attention you directed toward those tense and painful spots has already been beneficial.

If you continue to do this every day, you get used to going within and aligning yourself with what is going on inside you, instead of letting your energy unconsciously be absorbed by the hectic outside world. By going within frequently, your connection with your unique, individual flow of energy becomes stronger and stronger, and your intuition becomes clearer. You are then able to stay more attuned to what suits you and what does not.

As a soul, you have chosen to incarnate in an earthly body. Through your incarnation – by becoming flesh and blood – you wanted to know yourself more profoundly. The more you are connected with the Earth and with your body, the more fully you are incarnated, and the more you are able to realize your soul's longings in the realm of Earth. Is it possible then to be only partly incarnated? Yes, it is. If it is difficult for you to feel your body and, therefore, to also have trouble connecting to your emotions, you are only partly incarnated. Part of your consciousness has not been fully anchored in your body and does not feel at home here, and this causes feelings of unrest, irritability, and insecurity.

There are spiritual traditions on Earth that encourage you to transcend the body and that place the realm of heaven in opposition to the realm of Earth. But heaven and Earth are *not* adversaries, just like soul and body are *not* opposites. These two realms are meant to complement and mutually enrich each other. The heaven you are looking for – the Home you *long* for – is present in all the cells of your body. The light you call God flows through all earthly creation. Your spiritual goal is about truly valuing the realm of Earth and not about transcending it. I welcome you and encourage you to use my healing powers for your self-realization.

## What can you do for the Earth?

I also want to tell you what you can do for me. Many of you would like to know this, because you are concerned about the condition I am in. If you ask me, Earth, what you can do for me, my answer is this: *accept me, appreciate me, enjoy me. This* is the call that sounds from my heart to you reading this. Bless me with your loving attention – I ask for your blessing. You are gods in the making, so do not underestimate the power of what you radiate with your consciousness. The moment you connect with a plant, an animal, a stone, you touch and influence their consciousness. You can treat an animal carelessly, for example, as a means to satisfy your needs, or you can treat it as a unique being who wants to be cherished as such. The way in which you approach the animal has a direct impact on its self-awareness and the way it feels about itself. If you bless it with your loving attention, with your spiritual knowing that you both are part of one great Consciousness, you awaken something in the animal. It will experience a gain in life force, health, and self-awareness, and it will develop a bond with you that will have a positive effect on you both. The same goes for all living creatures in nature. When you hold a flock of birds in the sky with a loving gaze, admire a colorful sunset, or feel thankful for a fine, nutritious meal, you bless the Earth with your love. *This is what I ask of you.*

Now, you may wonder whether it can be really so simple and if you are really helping the Earth by being this way. It may seem that by only appreciating and blessing the Earth, you are doing nothing really about the pollution of the air or the water, the climate changes, and the other negative developments you take note of in the media. However, I say to you: *I am a living consciousness.* I am affected by your inner attitude toward me; I am a sensitive being, not a thing. Your blessings reach deep into my heart and I am better able to regenerate myself if you make an inner connection with me. From this connection, I can communicate with you and also tell you what you may do for me in particular. The most important first step, however, is to make the connection. This is not something self-evident in your culture.

Connecting with me is also connecting with your body. Your body is a part of the Earth, and I speak to you through your body. Many of you dislike your body. You do not approve of the way it looks, you resent the physical complaints it can give to you, or you simply feel caught in and restricted by your body. Because of this attitude, no message can come to you from your body. You first need to recognize and appreciate your body as the refined and unique instrument it is. *Your body is your closest friend.* It reacts to everything you think, feel, and sense. It is the mirror of your soul and wants to help you manifest your soul on the Earth. If you are able to feel this, and to let go of your judgments about your body, the inner connection can be made.

Once that inner connection is there, you will probably change some things on the outer level, too. Perhaps you will eat, breathe, or exercise differently and create more quiet time for yourself. You will, in any case, treat your body with more respect and probably want to go into nature more often. When these outer changes in behavior are born from an inner connection with your body, the changes will be lasting and will give you joy and satisfaction. It is of no use *forcing* yourself to change your behavior with regard to your health, or with regard to the environment. But when you approach problems of the body or problems of the Earth from such an external point of view, you are coming from your head and you are approaching them as if it were a battle.

As an example, think of what happens when you are on a diet to lose weight. If you do this from an external approach, from your head, you start from the idea that your body is not good enough as it is. It is fat, ugly, or unhealthy and "that has got to change!". You are expressing a contempt for your body as it is. Sticking to the diet will then depend on your will power and your ability to subject your body and your emotions to your will, and diets done this way usually fail. This approach is not born from a sense of respect for your body as it really is and for you as you actually are. A change of eating habits can only succeed if you work together with your body; if you can first accept it as it is and also be forgiving and loving about your emotions regarding eating. If you bless your body with your appreciation and respect, even if it does not comply with the many ideals and demands it is supposed to meet, it will start to tell you what it needs to be healthy. A unique flow of communication will arise between you and your body; a love relationship that helps you to realize your deepest potential.

It is the same in your dealings with me, Earth. I ask you first and foremost to see and recognize me for who I am. Revel in my beauty and take in my abundance. I am a reflection of you, just as is your body, so enjoy what I have to offer. Have faith in my power and my ability to self-heal. *You do not have to*

17

*save me, I am perfectly able to save myself.* I know who I am and I trust the Cosmic Powers who accompany me. My spiritual essence is indestructible and I do not fear annihilation by human hands. You do not support me by being angry and worried about the damage done to nature on the Earth. You help me by taking up your natural role in relation to me. In that role, you are both child and parent, both small and vulnerable *and* great and majestic. Allow yourself to be a child again who entrusts itself to the great Powers of life who carry, cherish, and sustain you. Dare to embrace your vulnerability and surrender to Powers who transcend you.

Yet be self-conscious, also, and accept your responsibility as a creator and inspirer of life. You are gods in the making, but you can only truly embody your divinity if you know yourself to *be* that and you are also connected with the great web of life that supports your very existence. Humility and surrender on the one hand *and* self-esteem and self-consciousness on the other are the qualities that reinstate the original role of giving and receiving between humans and Earth. I invite you to dance with me. Dancing together, heaven and Earth will merge and miracles will abound.

## Paradise lost

I am the voice of Earth. I have known you forever; your every footstep is felt and acknowledged by me. At the deepest level we are one because there is one consciousness that envelops us both. This consciousness is majestic and unnameable – it is the spirit of God. It is mysterious, yet at the same time, deeply familiar. Within the hand of this creative Consciousness, a game unfolds and we play this game together. We are partners in a relationship that has evolved over time. This relationship is now ready for transformation because we are entering a new era. But first, I will tell you more about the beginning of this game, the unfolding of our cooperation together. It is different from what you may have previously understood.

At our first coming together, you were not yet human; you did not possess a physical body. You were not yet incarnated on the Earth – you were an angel. *And you were not just any angel!* You belonged to a family of angels who intended to pave the way for a new adventure in the cosmos. And what was this adventure to be about? I will put it in very simple terms. In the cosmos, there is a law that says that "like attracts like". For instance, after you die when on the Earth, you are drawn naturally to an area in the spirit world that mirrors your state of consciousness. Your surroundings are a direct reflection of how you feel inside; *there is unity between inner and outer.* In the spirit world, there are realms of light and realms of relative darkness, and these realms are separate, but that is not the case on Earth, or so it appears. On Earth, many different types of consciousness are present at the same time and interact with one another. There is great diversity here, and therefore the Earth is like a huge melting pot of different realms of consciousness.

However, even here on Earth, it is the case that you create your own reality by your inner state of consciousness. And this is something you come to gradually understand in the course of a deep spiritual quest. At first, you are greatly distracted by an external world on the Earth that does not seem at all to be created by your own mind. On the contrary, you seem to be the product of that reality, rather than its creator. In the spirit world, the unity between inner and outer is simply a given: perceptible and palpable. But on the Earth, it takes a highly evolved consciousness to realize that state of unity and oneness, and to take responsibility for oneself as its creator.

On the Earth, a special experiment is taking place. When you are here in physical form, a veil is put over you so that you do not recognize your own divine creative power. It remains there until you awaken and see that you *are* God at the core of your being. Then the veil drops and you recognize the deep underlying oneness that pervades all living creatures on the Earth. The process of awakening on the Earth is intense and the very existence of Earth gives a powerful evolutionary impulse to the entire spirit world. In the spirit world, especially, there can be a lack of dynamics and of change. Indeed, a sort of stagnation or lack of development *has* taken place because all the realms are so completely separate.

Change, growth, and evolution occur when you meet and confront *otherness.* And when I speak of this meeting with otherness, I do not mean having a polite chat with it, but rather truly plunging *into* it. You learn and grow from diverse forms of consciousness, and not by studying them "from above", but by *becoming* them. This is exactly what happens when you plunge into incarnation on the Earth. You take a dive into the deep, and by incarnating, you connect to diverse realms of consciousness. This is how you forge a bridge between realms of being that would not have otherwise connected.

Being human means to be that bridge between widely diverse realms of consciousness. In the forging of that bridge lies the hope for an expansion of consciousness in all the realms of the spirit world. Even the highest evolved realm in the spirit world gains an impulse of growth and renewal from the great experiment on the Earth. Humans are able to explore the extremes of both light and dark, and eventually recognize the oneness behind all forms and appearances. And when human beings *do* attain this consciousness of oneness within themselves, they become conscious creators on the Earth, and their presence has a transformative and healing effect on all living creatures with which they come into contact.

# When humans were angels

Creating unity consciousness is the goal of your adventure on Earth. I started this story by mentioning that when we first began this process of cooperation, you were not yet humans, but angels. Your consciousness had not yet joined itself to any material form and you felt strongly connected with the other angels around you: your brothers and sisters. There was such a strong bond among you that you experienced yourself as the cells of one organism. You worked for a common good in a selfless, open way, being of the same mind and heart. And at a certain point, you heard a call from Earth. You were invited to embark on a journey with this planet.

But why you? To make a long story short, you were the bold ones among the angels. You were fearless, passionate and, yes, somewhat rebellious and self-willed. The claim has been made that you were banished from paradise because of your desire for knowledge and your willfulness. And yes, you were indeed curious and also a bit headstrong. *But that was precisely as it was supposed to be!* Do you think God made a mistake in creating you? No, God knew exactly what it was doing and, by the way, God does not deem anything wrong or sinful. God is perfectly capable of living with your "sins" – you are the ones suffering most from them.

Although it is understandable that you, as a human being, may regret some of your acts, it is not wise to be endlessly weighed down by them. In this respect, you have suffered a lot from your religions which have put such a strong emphasis on guilt and punishment. God is more gentle and compassionate than you would ever deem possible. You are forgiven even before you trespass. God whole-heartedly grants you the freedom to make mistakes and prefers that you look upon your mistakes with equanimity rather than that you chastise yourself about them.

All those "mistakes" are steps on the journey within, the journey on which you get to know yourself fully. And this journey is not straight; in fact, it is *meant* to be circuitous. Without twists and turns, there is no experience, and without experience, no awakening. You first have to get lost in order to again find Home, consciously. You were the ones taking the experience of "lostness" fully upon yourself, with the passion and the self-willfulness that God planted in your hearts. However, I am straying a bit from my subject!

Once you heard the call from Earth, you entered my realm. You found a planet rich in vegetation, with green forests, endless oceans, and a burgeoning animal kingdom. You were moved by the beauty and richness of life upon me. You felt encouraged to participate in this life, to inspire and nurture it with the angel energy that was at your disposal. I was happy with your arrival. You were my caretakers and you helped to take care of the life here and even implanted seeds of change and innovation into the existing life forms. How did you do this? You were so close to the source of creative power that you had magical abilities, as one would call them today. You allowed yourself to imagine new, exciting life forms, and these imaginings grew into spiritual seeds that attached themselves to already existing life forms. You impregnated life with new ideas and that is how biological evolution came to be.

All life forms are born from Spirit: *physical, material forms are the manifestation of spiritual forces*. Conscious spirit is much stronger than you assume. You have been raised with a materialist mind-set, which tells you that the physical – as described by the science of physics – is the foundation of reality. In fact, the opposite is true. Spirit is not the product of soulless matter; all matter is imbued with a creative consciousness that sustains it.

## Remember the angel within you

Let yourself go with your imagination for a moment. Remember who you were in those ancient times. It is possible for you to do so, for your soul is open and unlimited and knows no space or time. Imagine that you float above the oceans and forests in a very refined and ethereal body. You feel enchanted by the beauty you see, by the adventure that is about to unfold here. See yourself as an angelic being guided by your joy, your passion, your inspiration. You feel as free as a child who can do anything it wants.

Now imagine that you gather up your powers to express your sense of joy and respect for life in a magnificent flower. Allow an image to come forth of a flower which especially attracts you. See its colors and feel them from within. Hear the flower's laughter welling up from its heart like little bells ringing – *it is like music to your soul*. Now pass on this image to me, Earth. Imagine how it falls into my womb and how it is nurtured there by physical and ethereal powers that help this spiritual seed gain material form. This is what you did in those ancient times. You let yourself be carried away by the flow of your inspiration and impregnated me with it – and I was receptive. I, the awareness present in this material realm, wanted to be impregnated and to absorb your thought forms.

Our partnership and cooperation stem from that time. It is the reason why you can be so moved by the beauty of nature and the innocence of non-human life forms. You are not only touched by their physical beauty, you are also reminded of the old connection between you and life on Earth, and the joyful game you once played. You made your contribution to the creation of many earthly life forms. As an angel, you were the spiritual parent of life on Earth. This is how deep and far your creative power reaches.

## The veil that falls

During the time of which I am speaking, there were also dark powers present in the universe who became fascinated with the flowering of consciousness on Earth. Dark powers are nothing but energies who are not yet aware of their divine nature and therefore believe they need something outside themselves to be whole and complete. These dark powers wanted to feed on the life forms on the Earth which radiated such vitality and life force. But as a reaction to the intrusion of these dark powers, you wanted to protect the life on Earth. Your emotions were much like those of a parent who wants to shield its child from danger. To meet and confront the intruders, you had to have denser bodies in order to live in a denser energy, one less tenuous and subtle than the realm of the angels.

Essentially, the intrusion by the darkness lit a spark of passion and a fighting spirit in you and this in turn drew you deeper into matter. The next step in your journey was for you to let go of being an angel and so you took the path of incarnation. And with this step, you, in a sense, lost your innocence. There was that moment of hesitation when you realized that by becoming more material, you would lose something very precious. You would lose your "angel wings", which symbolize freedom from time and space, freedom from birth and death, and freedom from fear and illusion.

Yet there was something that deeply attracted you to the adventure of incarnation. You were a passionate and bold angel, as I said, and that was as it was meant to be. It would appear that your journey took a negative turn when you let go of being an angel and engaged in a battle with the dark forces, because you became involved in several conflicts and wars for a long, long time. However, this plunge into the deep made it possible to spread your angel energies to the farthest corners of the universe. Your angel energy is an unalienable part of you that, even if it is temporarily veiled, can never be taken away from you.

Your first mortal bodies were not made of physical matter as you now know it on the Earth. They were much less dense and solid; one would not be able to see them with human eyes. And your consciousness was less focused than it is now. You were able to go in and out of your physical forms easily and you experienced reality in a way that is similar to how you now experience the reality of the dream state. You were less aware of yourself as a separate entity: your "I-ness", as opposed to the outside world.

Presently, you are very much joined to your physical form, and many of you think you *are* that form and that you will perish with the physical body. But in your earliest incarnations, this was not yet the case, and in many ways you were much freer to go and do what you pleased than now. Nonetheless, you did feel confined and confused. Although you were guided by the intention to struggle for light and to protect life, you also had to now deal with dark emotions such as fear, desolation, and doubt. As soon as you start to battle someone or something, you cannot but partly absorb your adversary's energy. If that were not to happen, there would be no common ground from which to start a battle and you would simply let go of the other completely.

As an angel, you had only high and elevated feelings: joy, enthusiasm, and a strong sense of connectedness. But when you went down the road of incarnation, an emotional body formed around your soul. This energetic body contains emotional reactions that arise when you do *not* perceive reality from the standpoint of oneness and connection. The feelings of the angels have their seat in the heart, but when incarnated, the emotions you experience are related to the lower three energy centers or chakras, which are located in your body around the solar plexus, the navel, and the tail bone. These three chakras form the ladder to incarnation and through them you trade the experience of oneness for the experience of duality. However, it is also through them that you go *up* the ladder and rise from duality to oneness. Your emotional body presents the greatest obstacle to inner peace and liberation, because it contains fear, sadness, and anger. Yet the way to freedom and enlightenment goes up *through* the emotional body and not alongside or around it. We will speak of this later.

## Incarnation on Earth

As your emotional body grew denser and heavier and you lost track of your origin, the possibility arose to incarnate as a human. You had already become widely traveled souls and had experienced both the light and dark aspects of life. And the energies of duality had taken hold of you, which means that, for a long time, you believe in the illusions it creates. If you live in duality, you believe deeply within yourself that you are alone, fearful, and powerless, and that you need something outside yourself to acknowledge, protect, and support you. It is from this notion that you start to exert power over others in order to hide your vulnerability. Or you may become too vulnerable and give your power away to another being who wants to feed on your life energy. Whether you are offender or victim in this game, the fundamental error you make is that you think you cannot experience wholeness within yourself. There is this emptiness you want to fill, either by being the boss or by being the slave.

This game is a very painful one, as many of you have experienced. In that distant past, there was a moment in which you strongly realized the consequences of this game of duality, and that was your moment of change.

You had experienced both extremes of the game and knew there was no real solution in either extreme. You knew something had to change, but you did not know what or how. You had become far removed from the original freedom and joy of the angel inside you, yet your emotional body held a memory, a longing for "home". You knew there was something you wanted to go back to: a state of being that would feel like heavenly bliss to you. So the longing in your emotional body now caused you to embark upon a new path. Having explored the extremes of duality, you now started to turn within, and this change in your consciousness created the impulse to incarnate upon Earth as a human being.

At that point, the human being as a biological life form already existed on Earth. When you entered that life form, however, you added something to it that made the human being less animal and more self-aware. Human biology is related to the animal kingdom, but the human being was forged by powers which do not spring solely from natural evolution on Earth. What separates man from animal is the ability to be self-aware. Through this ability, the human being is able to transform their emotional body and to consciously spread the energy of the heart on the Earth. Whereas the non-human realms of nature unconsciously radiate the joy and connectedness of the angels, it is humanity's mission to transform that joy and connectedness into a conscious energy.

By incarnating into the human form, as it then existed on the Earth, you added something to its development, but this addition is paradoxical. On the one hand, self-consciousness holds a great promise, but on the other hand, it can lead you astray. By becoming human on Earth, you hoped to reconnect with all life on the Earth and to be the gentle creator and keeper you once were. Being human is a rich and complicated reality. Many aspects of reality come together in the human being: you are partly mineral, plant, and animal; yet also partly cosmic being with a long galactic history. Human beings are both dark and light, the lost ones and the redeemers, the cause of suffering and destruction, and, at the same time, the messengers of hope, love, and creative power. In the human being, many powers converge with the purpose of reconnecting and cooperating. The consciousness of the human holds the possibility to connect widely diverging realms of being and to reinstate the notion of underlying unity. Because of the possibility of realizing this beautiful ideal, humanity is granted the opportunity to make grave mistakes.

The goal can still be attained – hope is not lost. In fact, in this age, hope rises as never before. Great changes are occurring in the collective consciousness of humanity. I just referred to a moment in the past in which you realized that your salvation could not come from the game of stealing energy or giving it away; that the solution lies in finding wholeness within. This insight is now germinating in the consciousness of humanity. It is only a seed, not yet a plant, but a change is at hand and something is awakening in the heart of humankind. The heart is the connecting link between the many realms of consciousness represented in a human being: the earthly, the galactic, and the cosmic. The call for peace and fellowship now resounds throughout all these realms and this collective call creates a wave of energy that engulfs me, Earth.

# Angels in human form

If you feel touched by my words, and recognize yourself in them, you are one who has heeded this call from your heart. You are someone who wants to contribute to the transformation of consciousness on Earth. I welcome you and wish to assist you. I am telling you this long story to make you aware of who you really are: an angel at the core of your being. Your growing self-awareness helps me. If you remember who you are, we can again have a partnership.

I see your longing and feel your home-sickness. I see you reaching out for the joyful and carefree state that was once so familiar to you on the one hand, and now seems so far and distant on the other. It is now time to return to who you are. It is time to climb that ladder and embrace your emotional body with your heart; to surround your pain, your sense of heaviness, your sadness, with the angel consciousness of lightness and compassion that is natural to you – *you can heal yourself.*

You are now becoming an angel who is able to hold its light in the densest realm of reality. You are becoming a conscious creator who has learned to manifest itself in realms both light and dark without losing itself in them. You are carrying a seed of consciousness that is transformative for your environment – *you are becoming a spiritual teacher*. A spiritual teacher is not someone coming down from the highest realms to explain to the ignorant what life is all about. A spiritual teacher is someone who has themselves gone though the darkness and reaches out their hand to another – not from above, but from a deeply sensed inner unity.

The adventure you, as a creative angel, started upon long ago is nearing its end. In this final chapter of your journey, you are especially invited to reconnect with me, the life form on which this experiment is taking place. Allow yourself to travel in your imagination and become the dreamer and visionary you once were. Own the greatness of what wants to manifest itself through you on Earth. Become again the angel who graciously entrusts itself to the magic of life. Let yourself be guided by what gives you joy and inspiration. The angel inside you wants nothing more than to become fully human – and it is by feeling one with that angel that you bring a piece of heaven onto the Earth.

## Connecting to Earth

I am the voice of Earth. I salute you all in joy. It warms my heart to experience your presence and your openness toward me. I long to connect with you; we are meant to develop together and jointly walk the road to a different, new world.

I would like to take you back to the very origin of our mutual connection and cooperation. I am a living creature, a conscious being who received you here on this planet in very ancient times. I was receptive to your arrival here on Earth and wanted to learn and grow through your presence. You are not from the Earth; you come from the stars. You carry a light within you that is new and inspiring to the Earth and to all the realms of nature here.

Let me explain. As a planet, I absorb light from outside myself. I take in light from the Sun, which warms me and helps me bring forth life on this planet. I am inspired by the great force of the Sun and I need it to create and sustain physical life on my surface. You are representatives from the stars, and you carry star light within your soul, which you bring to the Earth when you are born here.

What is the meaning of this star light descending to Earth? What is the intention behind your coming? You are here to bring the light of consciousness to me and to all the realms of nature. You are here to awaken us to inner life. Whereas the physical Sun helps me to create and sustain physical life on Earth, your star light helps me, and all of nature, to grow and evolve in consciousness.

To offer a simple illustration of this process, think of what happens when you hold a flower in your hand and look at it in awe and with admiration. You see the exquisite beauty of the flower; you sense its purity, marvel at its colors, and enjoy its scent. The flower itself is not aware of its beauty; the flower is simply being itself. But because of your admiration, your presence, and your consciousness enveloping the flower, something awakens within it. She will start to experience herself as something beautiful and valuable. She enjoys your attention and a spark of conscious soul light awakens within her.

You will see that the plants and flowers to which you give conscious attention, simply by your enjoying and caring for them, will grow more abundantly, have more life force, and develop stronger roots into the Earth. You are creators, and by your thoughts, intentions, and self-consciousness you are able to add life force and creative power to nature here on Earth. This is exactly what nature longs to receive from you. All the realms of nature seek to grow in self-awareness, to reach out to the stars, to make that connection, and to absorb conscious star light within themselves.

Think of the animals, your pets you keep in and around your home. So many of you have a special bond with them. Whenever you enter into an intimate relationship with an animal, you receive their unconditional love and loyalty. The animal, however, also receives something from you in return. The animal is touched by your human presence and the particular type of consciousness that belongs to humans. Your presence lights a spark of consciousness in their being and that helps them evolve in their evolution toward greater self-consciousness.

Everything in the universe is growing and evolving toward self-consciousness. Self-consciousness brings one closer to the awareness of one's own divinity and indestructible light and creative power. Everything in the universe is gradually growing toward a state of consciousness in which it realizes: "I am a part of God – I am a creator myself". *To celebrate your divine creatorship and to handle it with responsibility is the purpose of Creation.* You are creators, and you as souls have come to the Earth to learn how to use your creative powers in a conscious and responsible way.

As creators, you are meant to contribute to my evolution and to inspire the realms of nature, which in turn provide you with many services and blessings on the material and energetic planes. But when you look at the current condition of the planet, it is hard to perceive there was once an original intention for a mutual cooperation between humans and planet. Things have not worked out as planned and many persons would say that things have gone wrong. In this moment, however, I ask you to remember your original excitement when embarking upon our mutual adventure. Your loving intention is still alive within your heart, even if you notice all around you that humanity has used its creative powers unwisely, and as a result, has damaged the Earth. One might say that humanity has veered off its course and taken a detour.

Originally, you came down to the Earth from a great source of light, like angel-children. You were innocent and pure, but as your journey progressed, you went astray. Humanity came to a point at which it refused to cooperate with the forces of nature and, instead, placed itself in opposition to nature. Humanity then lost its connection and roots to the greater whole. Out of fear, people sought to gain power over others, and over nature, in order to secure a place for themselves on the Earth. One could say a fall from Paradise took place. Where you had originally intended to serve the life on Earth, to nurture and inspire it with your creative powers, you now experience the opposite. You can see, in this present time, what happens when nature is no longer recognized as a living partner in creation.

Humanity's lack of respect for nature and the planet deeply saddens many of you. There is sadness in me, too, about all that has happened. The realms of nature – animal, plant, and mineral – have absorbed a part of the darkness and negativity spread by humanity. They have experienced in their own way a sense of abandonment, a crack in the all-pervading sense of oneness that once was. Yet, in the very heart of me, there is a lasting love and compassion for you all, and I ask you to also feel compassion for yourself and the whole of humanity. You are involved in a grand learning process and, as in any such process, it is inevitable that mistakes are made. It is a part of growing and learning that you embark on detours and dead-ends.

But now, in this age, the collective consciousness of humanity is changing. There are now more and more people who carry in their hearts a remembrance of the original bond between humans and nature. They have a silent awareness of the true and blessed relationship into which humans are meant to enter with me, their home planet. Feel again how deeply you are connected with my being.

*I love you so!* You are my angels of light and my faith in you has not withered. I ask you to acknowledge me and to allow my energy to pour through you again. I am a living partner walking right beside you on your path of incarnation on Earth. By connecting yourself more intimately with me, and by *grounding* yourself more, you bring your star light deep into the material realm. Letting your light shine and radiate will bring the changes on Earth so desperately needed right now. By connecting to me from your heart, your true self comes out. Every human being has a unique contribution to make to this grand adventure. Your unique gift inspires me, adds life force to nature, and inspires other people as well.

## What is grounding?

I would like to say more about the meaning of *grounding*. What does it mean to be grounded, to be connected to the Earth? Being grounded means being present in your body and being able to feel your body from the inside-out by feeling the flow of life in every part: from your head, to your toes, to your fingertips. Check for yourself if you can experience this flow. Can you feel your fingertips at this moment? Your toes? Can you feel the life inside them? Being grounded means you anchor your star light, your *soul* light, deep into matter, and the part of the material world closest to you is your body. The cells and molecules of your body are open to receive your light, your soul. *You are the sun for your own body.* Your consciousness makes your body alive and imbues it with healing power, life force, and vitality.

The anchoring of your soul into your body gives you the strength to fulfill your truest desires in life. Be aware of your creative power. The more you anchor your power into your body, the more you truly incarnate on Earth and create the changes in your life which you long for. When you are grounded, you feel clear and quiet. You are open to your soul's inspiration and, at the same time, you are connected to all that happens around you in everyday life. Becoming the bridge between cosmos and Earth, feeling that connection, is what it means to be grounded.

Many of you carry your soul light in the upper half of your body, around your heart and head. You find it difficult to let it truly descend into the lower part of your body: your abdomen, legs, and feet. One reason why this is hard for you to do is the fear of your own greatness. You have a fear of being the radiant angel and star that you are and to make a difference in the world. This fear is old, and its roots extend beyond this lifetime. In the past, you have incarnated on Earth many times and you have often felt unwelcome, but you are all in the process of healing this old pain.

I will suggest two ways of grounding yourself and feeling that you are indeed welcome on Earth, with your greatness, your creative power, and your divinity.

## Grounding through enjoyment

The first way is through enjoyment. You are not really used to enjoying yourself. Enjoying what? *Everything you can experience on the Earth.* Your body offers many possibilities for enjoyment, although many of these have been deemed sinful or inferior by your culture. You can enjoy the movements of your body, the sunshine on your skin, eating and drinking, the warm touch of another.

Being able to enjoy these things has to do with being able to truly *receive*, so why is this so difficult for you? Many of you feel there is something wrong with you, that you are somehow not right the way you are. You feel you have to achieve and work hard in order to receive acknowledgement and approval. This is an absurd idea, seen from the perspective of nature. Have you ever seen a wild animal work hard to gain recognition? No, the animal simply *is* and takes its right to be for granted, not as something it must deserve. The animal is able to enjoy without reserve – the sun, food, a water bath, the seasons and the natural rhythms of life.

You are all encouraged to *receive*, and to experience yourself as a divine being who is allowed to receive simply because of who you are. You are encouraged to enjoy the simple things that life in a body has to offer you. Receiving seems to be easy, but it is not. It requires a deep level of self-love and a deep recognition and appreciation of who you are. *Dare to reach out to that level of self-love!* Choose a moment every day in which you ask yourself what you can do for yourself now that truly gives you pleasure and fulfills you. What do you really feel like having or doing? *Then do it!* Do it for yourself, because you honor yourself and because you are here on Earth to enjoy yourself.

When you truly enjoy – whatever it may be – without guilt or shame, you are grounded. You are completely present in the *now* moment and all is well. There are no thoughts of the past or the future. Enjoying is being in the *now*, fully grounded.

## Grounding through creating

The second way of becoming more firmly connected to Earth, and being more grounded, is the way of creativity. *This is what you are made for.* Every human has a natural longing to express themselves and to manifest themselves in the world, which has nothing to do with achieving fame or success in society. Rather, it has to do with finding a way of expressing yourself that gives you real satisfaction. It may be the case that raising a family deeply fulfills you, or that leading a company inspires you. Perhaps caring for animals in some way is your heart's desire, or it may be a type of artistic expression that feels natural to you.

Every soul longs to express itself in some manner. The moment you respond to that longing, you feel fulfilled. The moment you allow the natural creativity inside to unfold, you feel: "Yes, this is me, this is how my energy wants to flow". In that moment, your soul connects to the heart of Earth, the heart of this reality. It is important to find out what you truly long for in your life and to make room for the creative flow inside you. This is where your divine essence touches the Earth and finds material form.

I now want to impress upon you all that you need to really stand up for yourselves more in this regard. Many of you suppress your impulses to do what your heart desires. So often you think: "How should I behave?", or "What is expected of me? What are my duties and responsibilities?". In this way, you will not find the key to the unfolding of your creative power. Your creative power speaks to you from your *gut*. It is not concerned with all the limiting rules and obligations that you have internalized. *Break free from these restrictions!*

Feel the fountain of fire and passion springing from your abdomen and let it flow freely. Sparks of light will find their way from your abdomen to your heart, and from the inside to the outside, and you will express yourself on Earth in your own original way. You will see that your creativity will touch other people and that it will make them more joyful and inspired. Following your passion and desire has a much more positive effect on the world than virtuously doing what you have been told to do, and forcing yourself to comply with limiting rules and structures.

This is a time of change. It is a time to be brave and take risks, to hear the voice of your heart and to act according to your heart in all areas of your life. By truly surrendering yourself to your heart's desires, you dig your roots deep into the Earth and you start to feel that life here is truly worth living.

## Full circle

The first way of grounding yourself is an incoming flow: receiving and enjoying. The second way is an outgoing flow: creating and giving. By creating from your heart, you give of yourself to the world. Receiving and giving, enjoying and creating, these together make a full circle and it is a *healing* circle. The more you dare to enjoy yourself, and to find yourself worthy to receive, the more you connect with your natural inspiration, the energy you are meant to share with this world. And as this flow of natural inspiration becomes stronger, and finds a creative form in the world, the more you enjoy the love and joy that will befall you on your path. The flows of giving and receiving, creating and enjoying, mutually reinforce each other.

I, Earth, also benefit from this healing circle of receiving and giving. In this flowing, dynamic circle, I work with you. It is my desire to nurture and stimulate your divine creative power: this unique spark within you. Human beings who have developed their capacity to enjoy and create will naturally enter into a different connection with the Earth. They will be aware of their greatness, their divine nature, and for that very reason will also understand that they are held and borne by a life force that connects all beings together.

Experiencing your own greatness also goes hand in hand with a sense of humility: the realization that your being is embedded in the great web of life that sustains *all* beings. Humans who honor and respect themselves naturally cooperate with their living environment: other humans, animals, plants – all nature. Knowing your greatness goes together with recognizing your place in the larger whole and deriving joy from the part you play in it.

I am also evolving toward a more expanded self-awareness. This new awareness has been awakened inside me, urged by both the good and the bad times on Earth. I am becoming more self-conscious and creative in my being. There is a longing in my heart for a reality in which humanity and Earth reestablish their original bond of love and companionship: a new Earth on which we joyfully cooperate. And where I am again inspired by your love and thoughtful attention, while I provide you with all you need when living in a physical body and attuned to the rhythms of nature.

## On a journey to a new Earth

I would like you to now travel with me to the future, to the new Earth. Imagine that the evolution we are now in together has progressed a few steps further. Let the new Earth that you all so long for be present in this moment. In our hearts, it is already alive as a seed, so let us nurture this seed with our consciousness and have it sprout in our imagination. See yourself living on this new Earth. What is the first thing you notice? Humans are living here in harmony with nature. Technology is used to support nature rather than manipulate it.

See whether you can find a home for yourself on this new Earth. There is a place and a community here in which you feel a part and belong. Let your imagination guide you and feel no restrictions when doing so. Where do you live on this new Earth? Can you find a natural surrounding in which you feel comfortable? Feel the environment and its climate, feel the ease and simplicity of life here. Life here is pure and simple, as it is meant to be.

Now take a look at what kind of work you do. Work means anything that inspires you and gives you a sense of fulfillment. What are you doing? You probably live in a small community of kindred spirits and you do exactly what your soul inspires you to do. What form does your creativity take? When you see or feel this, know that your soul is speaking to you in the present. What you are seeing is something that you long to do right now and something you *can* do right now, if only you trust and dare to be who you are. This is the work of your heart.

Now in this imagination of the new Earth, also feel what it is you truly enjoy. Let your inner eye provide you with a situation in which you truly enjoy yourself and receive something of what the Earth has to offer to you. Let an image of what that is spontaneously well up in your mind. What is it that truly makes you feel: "All is well and I am content." Feel the flow of giving and receiving in this place, this new reality, and hold on to it when we go back to the present. Earth is in a transition stage and the more people remember what their inspiration is – what they are here to give and to receive – the sooner the new Earth will be here.

## *Embracing your own nature*

Dear human child, I am Earth speaking to you. I am your mother and I bear you your whole life long. You are cherished by me, even if you are not aware of it because you are so absorbed in your day-to-day affairs. I encourage you to connect with me, as I wish to stir your memory and remind you of something old and precious, which in the modern world seems to have been forgotten. It is about the natural safety and security of being on Earth.

To be reminded of what that natural security of being on Earth is like, you only have to look at the whole of nature around you. Watch the seasons, how they come and go on their own, see the plants and animals go about their daily life, listen to the rustle of the wind or the murmuring of water. In this way, you are briefly reminded that the most important things in life happen spontaneously as a result of nature running its course. Nature is around you, as well as in you, for *your* nature is a part of the whole of nature.

You have become so accustomed to living from your head, especially those of you in the West, that you have forgotten you are a natural being, like the plants and animals. Look at the animals, how naturally they give themselves to life – they almost cannot do otherwise. They also have emotions, such as fear and resistance, but they do not oppose life as do humans. Human beings do, by excessive thinking, create a cage around their own nature, which eventually causes problems for them. Life cannot be organized and controlled by human thinking. The primal forces of nature are more vast than that, and sooner or later you will discover that for yourself. There will come a moment in which you have to give over control to nature.

You can reach such a moment through a crisis, or a situation in which you feel you have lost control, either internally or externally. And losing control is usually painful and can be a struggle for you, yet it will bring you Home. You might think you are lost and drowning in chaos, but you are actually coming closer to the natural security of Being itself. *Life holds and loves you*. Crises can appear to be cruel and unjust, but in truth they always carry, within them, nature's, or if you prefer, God's invitation that says: "Come Home, come back to me". There is a guiding hand within the crisis that seeks to support you and show you the way.

All who read this are on the inner journey to wholeness and completion of the self. You are seeking to bring your soul alive in a human body of flesh and blood. On this path, the soul descends into the body in different stages.

## From head to heart

When you have only started the inner path, you will probably have become acquainted with it through your head. For example, you may have become attracted to certain books which throw a different light on ideas and values you have always taken for granted. You may be disturbed by these new thoughts, yet strangely attracted to them, and it will fascinate you to read more about them.

This is how the journey within begins for many: you devour spiritual books like they are sweets. From deep within you, something wants to awaken and to change, and this first translates as the need for a new way of thinking. You then let go of some of the more rigid structures of your thinking and open up to something new. Speaking to other like-minded people can also be a helpful incentive in this process.

However, after some time, you start to long for more. You start to think: "Well, I understand what they're talking about in those books, but how do I apply all this to my own life? How does this knowledge come alive in me, and how do I truly translate it into feelings and actions on Earth?" This question may haunt you and drive you to despair, but you cannot force life. Yet, at a certain moment, something will happen in your life that will help you make the breakthrough from head to heart, and it is often some kind of crisis. Changes may occur in the area of work, relationships, health, or by the loss of a loved one. Whatever it is, at a certain moment, feelings will arise inside you which are so intense they cannot be ignored; you have to allow them in and let the transformation take place. That is when your soul incarnates more deeply into your heart.

First, your soul descended into your head, inspiring you to take in new ideas through books, talks, etc. Then the soul knocks at your door at a deeper level, the level of feeling. You will get acquainted with layers of emotions you never knew existed before. Crises spur these on and make old emotions from childhood come to the surface, perhaps even memories from before this lifetime. You will explore these layers of emotions and this is how the center of your heart opens up. Your soul incarnates even more deeply, filling the heart chakra with its energy.

The transformation that takes place at that stage may give rise to several complications. You start to look at the world through different eyes, and that causes your relationships with other people to change. Deep within you, the awareness of oneness awakens, which means that you come to realize that all of us: human, animal, plant, mineral, are all held together by a divine force, and that we are bound to one another, each a mirror for the other. This awareness can be overpowering and for many of you the breakthrough from head to heart causes a great sensitivity inside. This "high sensitivity" may create imbalances, because boundaries with others get blurred. You may take in a lot of other people's emotional energy, not knowing how to release it, and that can cause your moods to go from very high to very low.

## From heart to belly

The breakthrough from head to heart, however, though powerful and essential, is not the last stage in the incarnation of the soul. The soul wants to descend even deeper, into the abdomen.

When your soul has descended to the level of your heart, you have partly awakened. You are aware of your feelings; you dare to look at your emotions; you are prepared to go within and face your inner wounds, but you also feel weakened and vulnerable by your high sensitivity and the instability that arises because of that. Because your heart is so full of feelings, you lose your grounding at times, and this can be difficult – this happens to many of you. When your heart center is opened radically, your sensitivity may become too much for you and you may want to withdraw from the world. You will no longer feel able to express yourself creatively, because it is all too much and too overpowering, and this can make you feel anxious and depressed.

*The answer to this problem is not in going back up into your head; the answer is going down into your abdomen.* You are ready for the next step in the incarnation process of your soul: the transition from heart to abdomen. Your soul wants to flow even deeper into your body. Within your abdomen is a space or point of silence; go there with your consciousness, now as I speak. In that space, there is no language, no thinking, no concepts. You may hear the rustling of leaves in the wind or the sound of the beating of waves, and those sounds can help you become aware of the silence that is within this space.

At this level, your spiritual knowing and feeling become instinctual, or as it is sometimes called, your "second nature". There is no need to understanding things through thinking or even feeling. A deep knowingness is present from which you act and life pours through you easily. Your soul has then become your nature, it has descended to the level of instinctual awareness. This gives you the balance you need to remain centered and calm even when in a demanding and turbulent situation.

Your heart, your feeling center, wants to connect with your abdomen in order for your heart to be truly grounded and for you to feel safe and secure on Earth, so let us together now visit that place in your abdomen. Trust that it is there, and tell your soul it is welcome there. Allow your soul to flow from your head – inspiring your thinking, to your heart – radiating love and kindness, to your abdomen – giving you trust, self esteem, and a profound inner knowing that you are *what you are* and that you are good *as you are*. Feel your abdomen opening up to you. Sense how the golden light of your soul flows down to your root chakra and connects with me, Earth.

Go deeply within, and *be* this center of silence. Know that from there, your high sensitivity will be balanced with peace and calm. In this balanced state, you will know how to put boundaries around your feelings, when to open up and when to keep your distance by staying close to yourself. You determine when to say "yes" and when to say "no", when to connect and when to let go, and the key to doing this is in your abdomen.

# An animal that helps you

To help you connect with this center, I suggest you imagine an animal that represents the inner power residing in your abdomen. Take the first animal that comes to mind. Remember that animals are very spontaneous creatures; they live from their instincts, their natural reflexes. This animal reflects *your* inner instinctual knowingness. It is already there; it is waiting for you. You do not need to create it; you need only to see and recognize it. Invite this animal to come near you – welcome it and look into its eyes. Ask whether it has a message for you that will help you to descend deeper into your abdomen. Let the animal speak, for this animal embodies the wisdom of the instinctual and you can receive that wisdom. And because you have a heart and a head, you can also feel and articulate that wisdom.

That is the beauty of the cooperation between head, heart, and abdomen. Not one of them is better or higher than the other; rather it is their balanced cooperation that makes you whole and complete. Your head can give you much pleasure. Thinking can be useful and fun, as it gives you the opportunity to communicate with others: it provides you with a common language. Your heart offers the possibility to experience joy and the whole range of emotions human life comprises – it is a beautiful gift. Your abdomen gives you your foundation, your I-ness, if that is a proper word. Your abdomen allows you to be really you, firm and rooted, established in your own boundary by using your discernment. From this foundation, the interaction with your heart and your head becomes a joyful play.

If these three layers of your being are aligned and integrated with one another, you feel whole, and life on Earth is worth living. It can be full of inspiration, love, and happiness. You can give yourself to what moves and inspires you, while at the same time not losing your foundation, your inner point of silence.

You can remain close to yourself, yet at the same time freely give and receive what life offers.

I salute you all. My love and compassion are always with you – we are playing this game together. You are beautiful and rich as human beings. Have faith in the beauty and power of the instruments given to you, the instruments of thinking, feeling, and being.

## *Surrender to your heart*

I am the voice of Earth. I am your foundation and I bear you by way of the body in which you are alive and living. I am part of your body, and the cells in your body are connected with me and carry in them my strength and vitality. My energy is a live stream that flows throughout your entire body.

Your body continually informs you about who you are and what is going on within you. Your body is the bearer of your feelings and your emotions, and it is by way of your emotions that your soul speaks to you. It is not easy for you to hear the voice of your soul speak through your emotions because you are accustomed to approaching life from your mind, but that approach goes against life. Life, in you and in me, is born from passion and creative power, and your mind can have no understanding of the dynamics of life without connecting itself with your heart and your abdomen.

In my previous message, I described how the light of your soul descends from your head, through your heart, and then into your abdomen, which is its final destination. It is only when the light of your soul descends fully into your abdomen, can your soul shape and form your life, your work, and your relationships. You then become more attuned to the rhythm of your soul and, in this way, life from your soul becomes your "second nature". Knowing is no longer something that lives only in your head and your emotions, it has now become an *instinctual knowing*. When the light of your soul descends that deeply into your being, an inner transformation takes place: you begin to radiate from the inside outward. This is the path that your soul encourages you to follow.

This period of time on Earth provides the possibility for you to take this path. This is a time in which the consciousness in many people is awakening; it is a time of acceleration and a time of making choices. When you choose to receive the unique light of your soul on Earth, you are choosing a path of descent from head to heart to abdomen. On this descending path, the area of your abdomen is of great importance because your deepest emotions are located there. It is there that your passions and desires, as well as your fear, anger, and doubt are alive. Many of you have already taken the first steps from your head to your heart. You have connected with your soul and your heart is open. Now, you are looking for an earthly way to manifest the inspiration that lives in your heart, and I see and feel your seeking. I *encourage* this seeking in you and in the next two messages, I will describe an inner journey to your abdomen. In this message, I will discuss the chakras that lie below your heart: the solar plexus, the navel, and the root chakras.

## A balanced ego

The solar plexus is the chakra center of your earthly "I": the personality that belongs to you, which is also known as the ego. The ego is an inseparable part of you as a human being. A balanced ego state keeps you connected with your heart and helps you, through thought and action, to turn the urgings of your soul into an earthly form. In that way, the ego is the link between the Earth and the soul. In many religious and spiritual traditions, the ego is seen as something negative. These traditions teach that the primal longings located in the abdomen are to be distrusted, and the aim of these traditions is to eliminate or to transcend the ego. I tell you that your passions are *not* a hindrance. They are an essential starting point for opening the way for your soul to descend onto Earth. The fire in your abdomen, when connected with your soul, is meant to become an inspiring torch of light for the world. This fire includes your emotions, your passions, your desires. It is *not* the intention that this fire be extinguished, but that it receive direction from your heart.

While religion is traditionally against the ego, the ego in your society is powerfully encouraged: ambition, success, and outer recognition count heavily. This emphasis on outward goals can make it difficult for you to find your own unique way. Before you are aware of it, your thinking and acting are motivated by external ideas that are often based on fear. A pursuit of success might stem from a deep fear of "not being good enough as you are" and the recognition of others seems as if it would take away this doubt, so you become dependent on external forces beyond your control. If you become fixated on outer values and approval, your ego becomes the "all powerful" force within you and you lose your connection with the larger whole. In this way, a "big ego" comes into being; one that struggles to maintain the edifice of success and respect, while your very foundation is being eaten away by fear and uncertainty.

The fire of the ego can be either weak or strong. In your world, you are encouraged both to make yourself "small", as well to make yourself "big". Religion preaches that you are sinful and insignificant, while society demands that you be attractive, productive, and successful. Most people have in their ego a mix of both tendencies. The one tendency is toward vanity and making themselves bigger, while the other tendency is toward docility and making themselves smaller. Seen from the perspective of the soul, neither tendency is healing.

Whether you have a strong or a weak ego, deep within, you feel fearful and abandoned because your ego is not connected with your heart. In both cases, the ego flounders in a morass of doubt. It does not take root in a fertile soil that provides nurturing and security. The feeling of being lost, which you have when your ego stands by itself, can be dispelled only through connection with your soul. No religious or worldly power can provide the security and connection needed to live in joy and confidence. Only the soul is capable of inspiring the ego from within so as to lift the ego out of its loneliness. This can happen only when the ego is willing to give up its separateness and surrender to something greater than itself. When you make the connection with the voice of your heart, the voice of your feelings, you open the gate between your ego and your soul.

## Listening to the voice of your heart

In order to recognize the path of your soul, it is important to live consciously with your everyday emotions and to ask within whether there is a message contained in these recurring emotions. If you listen to your emotions and consider them as messengers, you relate to yourself differently than in the way that you have become accustomed. You now have a tendency to condemn your feelings and to push them aside, so there is much that you deny yourself. Yet your emotions often tell you about an inner desire that wants to be seen and heard; a desire for a deeper, fuller, and more creative life in which you have meaningful relationships with others. Your response to this desire is usually twofold. On the one hand, you hear the call of your soul, but on the other hand you push that call away, because it is asking you to break with acquired certainties, habits, and expectations. Your soul wants you to stand up and to live from your own truth, yet this urging can make you fearful. You are afraid to let go of certainties; afraid to deviate from the norm and to come into possible conflict with the world around you. Because of these inner doubts, many of you hesitate on the brink of a real breakthrough into your actual destiny.

However, life does not stand still – it propels you forward. Life is asking of you to choose the voice of your heart, over and over again. What finally helps you over the threshold appears most often in the form of a crisis. Disease, burn-out, job loss, death of a loved one, or a relationship breakup set adrift all your certainties. In such a crisis, life seems to become rudderless. Your ego, your earthly personality, finds itself face to face with forces it cannot control. This puts a choice before you: do you resist or do you let go? At such moments, life provides an opportunity for you to really open up. In a crisis, an inner breakthrough can take place. However, this requires of you that you let go of preconceived expectations about your life by giving up what you thought you had secured.

A crisis brings loss into your life, yet at the same time space is created for something new. In a crisis, you are compelled to connect with your deepest feelings and to be consciously present in this flow. A crisis calls for great inner strength, because what is happening is often not agreeable to the ego. It will resist and panic, and not want to linger in the emotions of fear and anger. During a crisis, the resistance to change is intensified, while at the same time you are deeply challenged to let go of the resistance and to jump in and to risk going deeper. When you dare to go with the flow of your feelings, without condemning them, the life force brings you to a new place under the Sun.

By saying "Yes" to what happens in your life, to your feelings and to this new movement, you form a channel between your heart and your solar plexus – the voice of your soul becomes audible. You open up to the deep and powerful emotions that well up in you and you treat them with respect. In this way, a consciousness arises in you that is in harmony with your unique energy; a consciousness that no longer focuses on outside rules and standards. In attuning to your own unique energy, your consciousness enters new paths. The paths you now follow will be chosen by your feelings and no longer by your thoughts. By feelings, I do not mean your emotional impulses that flutter up with every change of the wind. I am referring here to an inner joy, an inspiration that fills your heart, so you know that it is good to make a particular decision.

# The heart as your guide

To choose from your heart means to decide from a quiet knowing: "this is good", without being able to explain why intellectually. What is important to realize is that the ego is not there to *make* choices, the ego is there to *give form* to your choices in the everyday world. The ego may seem to be more rational than the heart, because it calls on the language of rational reasons and common knowledge and standards, but, in fact, the ego does not *want* to differ from the known and predictable. However, when you base your life on external influences, you are not really *living*, you are being *lived*. This will gnaw at you and bring inner turmoil.

To make decisions from the heart may seem scary, and the choices you make are sometimes difficult to explain to others, and even to yourself. Yet this is the only way forward, when once you have chosen to embody the unique light of your soul on Earth. Once you have taken this step, you will end up in a different life stream. From the flow of rationality, you enter into the flow of synchronicity. The word synchronicity here refers to the surprising and positive events that suddenly take place effortlessly in your life: encounters that truly "connect", and opportunities that appear from nowhere. Whatever you need and want to enrich your life comes spontaneously onto your path.

This synchronicity cannot be explained from the rational viewpoint of the world, because the flow of synchronicity is essentially nothing other than "the rhythm of your soul". When you live from the rhythm of your soul, miracles happen in your life. When you listen to your soul and you do not push and shove against life, events and meetings happen spontaneously on your path that help you to radiate the light of your soul on Earth. You do less, and you simply allow more things to just happen. Your ego is no longer the "captain of the ship"; it has given over the wheel to your heart. Your solar plexus lets you be inspired by the voice of your heart and, in this way, creates the bridge between soul and Earth.

From the perspective of the soul, coincidence does not exist. The good that you attract when you live from your heart is a reflection of your confidence, joy, and imagination. Your soul is, in a manner of speaking, throwing valuable gifts to you from the boundary of Heaven. The question is whether you can receive these gifts. Is your heart open and your mind sufficiently empty? Can you live without expectations? Can you be thankful for what you have, even though there is still much you miss and there remains a desire in you for "more" and "different"? To allow yourself to be moved by your soul, surrender is required – *a leap into the vast unknown.*

People are accustomed to trying to force and control life, which produces problems for many in the area of their solar plexus. This expresses itself, for example, in stomach complaints, which are the result of stress and tension. The center of your ego can become stimulated by your need to control life and this need can never be fully satisfied and, therefore, creates a lot of tension and unrest within you. In this way, life is at odds with the flow of trust and surrender that is necessary in order to feel the rhythm of your soul. On the path of descent of the soul through to the abdomen, the light at the solar plexus is often blocked by an excessively active will that tries to give form to life from a restrictive tunnel vision. Often a profound crisis is needed to break open this tunnel vision. This is not to mean that you *have* to wait for a crisis in your life before you begin to listen to the voice of your heart and the rhythm of your soul. If you are aware of your own tension and unrest, then there is already a space opening for change in your life.

How can you increase this space? How can you create sufficient space to receive the light of your soul? I offer three suggestions that can shed light on your path:

## 1. Tune in to your unique path

Realize that your path is unique. Choosing from the voice of your heart is always choosing what wants to express itself from within, while your ego usually lets itself be guided by what is required or expected from without, or in order to be appreciated by others. Choosing your own way means that you let go of these motives and allow yourself to be guided by a truer source of leadership: *the voice of your soul.* How do you know when you are connected with your soul? Connection with your soul gives you a sense of joy and inspiration. The voice of your soul tells you to believe in your deepest desires and your wildest dreams and, at the same time, the inner guidance of your soul remains focused on the earthly embodiment and manifestation of these dreams and desires. In your everyday life, you get opportunities continually to realize the ideals of your heart, and to do that step by step. Through this process, you become challenged constantly to trust your unique path: do you choose from your heart or do you choose from a fear that is motivated by dictates from your ego?

## 2. Dare to surrender

Dare to surrender to the wisdom of your heart and to realize that surrender is a *creative force*. Sometimes you think that creating means you must focus your thoughts on a particular purpose, whereas creating something new means precisely the opposite: that you let go of all such thoughts – *the new lies beyond the known*. If you are trying to attract or create a new reality by way of your thoughts, you limit life in what it is able to give to you. You do not often realize that you are thinking from a tunnel vision, because you are not aware of *how restrictive are the ideas that you carry within yourself*. Truly creating is opening to the possibilities of the *unknown* and not fixating on a predetermined purpose. *Dare not to know!* To surrender to your heart is to be open to something new and fresh that you cannot yet entertain with your mind, and this surrender is not a "passive letting go". It means relying on the power of your desires and dreams, and placing your human hand in the hand of your soul and relying on *its* guidance. In that state of alert receptivity, you respond to the signals you receive from the flow of your feelings.

## 3. Honor the natural rhythm of your soul

When you align yourself with the voice of your heart, and you listen to your gut feelings and do what gives you joy and inspiration, you begin to recognize the rhythm and timing of your soul. This rhythm is sometimes not easy to follow and the timing is almost always slower than what you would wish for with your human will and thinking. Often, the realization of your soul's desires on Earth means that you must first see their dark and fearful sides. For your human consciousness, this is difficult to understand and there may be moments in which you lose all hope and confidence. And it often happens that form is given to your original desires only after you have almost given up on them – *the way of the soul is one of seeming detours*. However, know that when the seed of your desire is sown it will eventually come to fruition. The road toward your desire becomes lighter and more joyful when you understand and appreciate the rhythm and timing of your soul. Have respect for the slowness that is particular to this path. Patience is a form of trust and testifies to inner wisdom.

## *Embracing your inner child*

I am Earth. I embrace you, gently and firmly, as a mother. From the ground beneath your feet, I bear and protect you. Allow me to give to you what you need. By opening yourself to me, you let the cells of your body take in my life force and energy.

I will now talk about the center of your emotions, the navel chakra, which is located in your abdomen. In my previous message, I described the descent of the soul to the level of the solar plexus, the third chakra, which is in the area of your diaphragm. Further down the body is the second or navel chakra, which sits in the middle of your abdomen, slightly below your actual navel, and this chakra is related to emotion, connection, sexuality, and intimacy. It contains your ability to experience deeply and intensely. This area can be a source of joy for life, for enjoyment, and for connectedness, but it can also be overshadowed by feelings of inferiority, fear, and loneliness.

On the path of the descent of your soul, you may discover that there exists within you a sense of emotional insecurity that stems from experiences of rejection in the past. As a child, you are very sensitive to the approval of your parents. Actually, as a young child, you consider your parents as gods: they are your creators who have brought you to Earth. They are the persons in your first years of life on whom you, as a child, are entirely dependent for your physical survival and your emotional well-being. How that relationship takes shape for you and how you experience it, will have a major influence on your self-image as an adult.

The fears you are experiencing in your current life are fears that are partly inherited from your parents, often at a subconscious level. Your basic beliefs about life on Earth are largely formed by them. These beliefs, and their accompanying emotional habits and reactive patterns, were transmitted through their words, actions, and appearance. You absorbed these impressions into every pore of your body when you were strongly associated with your parents during your early childhood.

# Letting go of your childhood

When you mature and consciously take the path of the descent of your soul, you choose essentially to be born anew – a second birth. This new birth means that you become aware of the unconscious views and fears concerning life held by your parents. You confront these views and fears by allowing the light of your consciousness to shine on them – *you take responsibility for your life*. You take the child within you under your *own* guidance and protection and you become your *own* mother and father. You "grow up", as it were, a second time, with new, empowering beliefs that lovingly replace the old insecurities and fears. You create a new security for yourself on the path of descent, which means you receive yourself unconditionally and with love.

Your abdomen is the area where you can emotionally experience the greatest empowerment of who you are as a human being. It is the center from where you intimately connect with others and from where you respond spontaneously and instinctively. In many of you, it is here where exist the negative beliefs that are basic about yourself, beliefs that can contain fear and uncertainty. For example: "I'm not good enough; I need to control myself; I need to work hard; I have thoughts and feelings that are wrong; I'm not worthy of love; I may not distinguish myself from others; etc." The central component in all these beliefs is the idea that *you are not good as you are and that you should do something in order to receive approval from the world.*

This is an idea that can easily develop within a child because you – like nearly all children – experience that your parents are not capable of giving you unconditional love. And as a child, you soon come to believe that you know the cause of this failure – *you, as you are.* The next step is that you believe you ought to be *other* than you are – better, more attractive, more successful – and that by changing your behavior you will gain your parents unconditional acceptance and love. You try all sorts of ways to earn this love, and it is because of this lack that a basic feeling of unworthiness and insecurity takes root in your abdomen

The painful part of this situation is that the promise of unconditional love from your parents can never be fully met. The truth is that you as a child *did not fail,* but that your parents, because of their own negative beliefs, cannot love themselves as they are and so they cannot express their love to you in a way that makes you feel fully accepted by them. In most cases, they themselves have never experienced unconditional love.

How can you break this chain of inherited lovelessness? How do you recognize where you are still stuck in the fears and uncertainties of your parents? In this message, I invite you to examine how the energies of your mother and father have influenced you, so you can see clearly in which areas you lack a sense of security and safety, and how you can give it to yourself.

## Letting go of your mother

The first intimate relationship in your life is the one with your mother. In the womb, you are physically and emotionally fully connected with her – you are hardly aware where you end and she begins. Her emotions and moods are the setting in which the seed that you are thrives and blossoms. Her womb is your dwelling place, your temporary "home", and it forms the gateway to life on Earth. Your mother is, in those early life stages, a symbol of the female. Although every human being carries both the female and the male energies, at the moment you become a mother, you are an expression of the female energy of Creation. You represent for the child in your womb the receiving, connecting, and nurturing aspects of the female energy. In this expression of the female by the mother, the beliefs that the mother has about herself and her femaleness will leave its stamp on her motherhood and her relationship with her child.

In the society and cultural tradition in which you grew up, the female energy is often undervalued. For a long time, the male energy has been deemed superior. The emotions and feelings, typically female energies, have long been regarded as suspect and less reliable than the intellect and thinking. Relative to human nature, the feeling and empathic approach to life is viewed as sentimental or childish, while rational, scientific knowledge is seen as "adult" and the best basis for action. There has long existed a struggle between the male and the female energies that has left deep scars in the lives of both men and women.

Both sexes have suffered the oppression of the female energy. Women were not allowed their strength, and men were not allowed to connect with their feelings. This way of being is disruptive to the balance between female and male energies in both men and women.

The ingrained beliefs that live in your culture about the female and femininity, and the male and masculinity, are naturally passed on by parents to every new child who is born. This chain can only be broken when women and men begin to experience for themselves that these beliefs are constricting and they consciously decide for a new way of viewing the interplay between the male and female energies.

What images of the female and femininity have you inherited from your mother? The female stands as the archetypal energy for empathizing, receiving, and connecting with another. The female energy is fluid, flowing, and inclined to reach out toward others; it represents in its highest forms the qualities of the heart: unconditional love, compassion, and mercy. Could your mother accept and embrace her femaleness as something beautiful and precious? Imagine how, as a small child, you rested in her womb. What do you feel first? What sense surrounds you there? Is there joy and connectedness? Or do you feel fear and worry? Allow what you missed in the womb to emerge spontaneously in you and give this to yourself at this time. Send it to that child from the *now*, and feel it being received. That child you see before your mind's eye still lives. It is present in *your abdomen* and waiting for *your love*. You can give it now, everything it lacked then.

## Letting go of your father

How was the relationship with your father when you were a child? Just as women, men have inherited a distorted image about the male energy, as well as about the female energy. Men are often required to repress their emotions. Acting "like a man" often implies that you maintain control, show no emotion, hide your vulnerability, and act decisively. This image of maleness and masculinity, synonymous with the unemotional, has deeply touched the soul of men, just as the undervaluing of female energy has inwardly wounded women.

How did your father experience his male energy and the demands that were put upon him as a man? Did he repress his sensitivity? Could he emotionally connect with you? Allow an image to come up of the both of you together. Imagine that you as a small child stand beside him and he holds your hand. What do you feel first? What does he radiate to you? Do you feel good and safe with your father? Is he emotionally present for you? Look at what you missed then and give the child who you were what it needs. Kneel down before the child and observe it. Let the child know through the look in your eyes that you are there for him or her and that it is safe and secure with you.

In its highest form, the male energy represents *conscious ego power derived from inspiration*. The healed male energy is honored when serving and protecting the female energy. Discernment, wisdom, a broad vision, courage, and self-awareness are the qualities of a balanced male energy. The one-sided emphasis on thinking and on dominating nature – both inwardly: your emotions, as well as outwardly: your environment – is replaced by a harmonious interplay between feeling and acting, and between inspiration and manifestation.

## Balancing the masculine and feminine within

In each person there is an interplay between the male and the female energies. No person is purely female or male, because your soul is neither male nor female. However, if you incarnated in a female body, then you are naturally more strongly connected to the qualities associated with female energy. When you are born in a male body, the qualities of male energy are more natural for you. During the process of your second birth – the path of descent that your soul undertakes in cooperation with your earthly personality – you will sooner or later encounter the question of how things stand in relation to this balance between male and female energies within you.

Only when both aspects are allowed to be present in your being and support each other will there be true emotional security in your abdomen. In practice, this means, as a man, that you may again feel at home with your emotions, your vulnerability, and your sensitivity, and, as a woman, that you discover your inner strength and dare to consciously inhabit your space. In general, on the path of descent of the soul, women are asked to take back their power, while men are asked to embrace their sensitivity and to connect again with their feelings.

Many women have been taught as girls that they can earn approval only by giving – giving understanding, care, and service. For the "searching-for-love" child, giving becomes a means of being accepted and appreciated. However, when giving is driven by the longing for unconditional love and emotional security, you soon begin to live an unbalanced life. You feel you *need* to give in order to feel good, because your self-esteem depends on it. This leads to giving without bounds and a loss of self in relationships. It leads to emotional dependency, whereby you chronically undervalue yourself and you eventually lose sight of inner beacons of security and safety. For many women, it is important that they find their strength and independence and dare to live for themselves. They benefit from the male energy of standing up for themselves and of setting boundaries in their relationships with others.

With men, the reverse is often the case, because showing your power is encouraged for boys. They are taught that to stand out, perform well, and excel are valued qualities. The "ego-force" is emphasized and the connection with others is de-emphasized: performance is the motto. Through this image of what is ideal, "guys" get the idea that it is good to suppress their feelings, which are linked to vulnerability and weakness. You get recognition through performance and by masking your vulnerability. However, through the crowding out of your feelings, you lose the connection with your soul. When outward performance is not supported by inner inspiration, you increasingly become alienated from yourself and eventually you live *only* for outward recognition and appreciation, and this creates a deep emotional insecurity. For men, connecting with their feelings and expressing their emotions is of great importance. In order to create a guiding light of emotional security within himself, it is healing for a man to create emotionally meaningful relationships with others and, in this way, allow himself to be guided by the female energy of the heart.

Restoring the balance between the male and female aspects within yourself is an individual path that you need to travel, and in this message, I have given some general guidelines. However, it is also quite possible that, as a woman, you are experiencing problems with daring to enter emotional relationships, while as a man you may experience problems with standing up for yourself and with setting boundaries. A woman, who naturally has a highly developed male energy, may experience resistance in surrendering to gentleness and intimacy. A man, who is naturally sensitive and feels at home with the female energy, can especially experience difficulty with standing up for himself and manifesting his ego-force. Often there is a mixture of both aspects present in people.

## Making yourself whole

In whatever way this striving for balance takes form, the fact that you have taken up this quest for wholeness testifies to your inner strength. By seeking this balance between male and female within yourself, you stop looking to others to be your ideal mother or father; for example, a parent, a beloved, a close friend, or a teacher. Deep in every human being *is* the longing for the ideal mother and father: the mother as a source of inexhaustible love, care, and understanding, and the father as an unconditional source of wisdom, support, and protection. This desire for the ideal mother and the ideal father is essentially nothing else than the desire for balance between the male and female energies within yourself.

When you begin the journey of inner awareness and growth, you will need to let go of the idea that someone else can be your ideal mother or your ideal father. Neither your earthly mother and father, nor a beloved partner can meet this expectation. Still, as an earthly being, you often project this desire onto the most intimate relationships that you have. The search for the ideal mother or father, who fully understands, accepts, appreciates, and loves you, is a primordial desire of the child in you that has been deprived of this love and is still experiencing the pain of that deprivation. It is your task as an adult to embrace this needy child within yourself with your own female energy of gentle nurturing and your own male energy of protection and wisdom.

No woman can embody the archetypal mother energy for you, and no man can give you the energy of the archetypal father. By letting go of this expectation, you liberate your relationships with others from a demanding pressure and heavy burden – *the release of your deepest inner pain* – something no other person can do for you. You let go of unrealistic and high expectations about others in order to make space for openness and flexibility in your relationships. You alone take upon yourself the responsibility for the needs of your inner child, and doing so allows the other person to be what he or she is: a human being with its *own* unique history and its *own* mixture of fearful and loving convictions.

Become your own mother and father by embracing the child within and giving back to it its *truth*. And that truth is that *you are good as you are*, that you are courageous, loving, and innocent in everything you think and feel, and that *it all already exists within you.* The more you support yourself from your own inner mother and father, the lighter, more joyful, and more creative the child within you will become. This knowledge will transform your relationships with others because you will no longer look to others for your emotional security. You will be secure and safe, in and with yourself, and therefore can be open to an emotionally intimate relationship with another person. Being independent and secure – *as you are* – means you have much to share with another, as well as being open to receive much from another. The love and friendship you receive from the other person will confirm what you already know – *I am good as I am.*

## *Feeling safe and secure in your body*

On the path of the descent of your soul, you come ever closer to me, Earth. The aim of your soul's journey is that *you completely connect with me.* Your soul wants to fully embody itself on Earth at *all* levels: the head, the heart, and the abdomen.

The root chakra, the energy center at the bottom of your spine, symbolically contains your "roots" in the Earth. It reflects your basic beliefs about life in a body on Earth and your ability to express yourself freely, securely, and safely in the material realm. In many people, there is a deep fear in the root chakra: *the fear of being fully present in the body and the feelings.* You feel that being fully present creates vulnerability, but that is not so. Because of painful memories from the past of rejection and of being hurt – both emotionally and physically – you have partly retreated from your body, especially from your abdomen, which is where you can experience severe emotional pain. Many people are not fully present in this part of their body because of emotional trauma they experienced in this life or in previous lives here on Earth.

It is possible that you experienced a lack of emotional security in the family in which you grew up. As described in the previous message, as a young child, you may have already come to believe that you need to be other than what you are, so you need to *earn* the love you are seeking. This makes it difficult, at the level of the solar plexus – the third chakra, to rely on the voice of your own heart and to let go of outer standards imposed upon you from the world around you. In addition, unprocessed traumas – painful soul memories from previous lives – can be playing themselves out in your current life, causing you to not have incarnated on Earth in a deep, heartfelt way. These painful soul memories can have resulted in "incarnational" pain at your birth, which made it difficult for you to get a good grounding and to feel at home in your body.

For many people, the unprocessed traumas from previous lives trigger and reinforce the emotional wounds from this life, causing both to become active in them. When you do not know how to heal the pain in your root chakra, or are barely aware of it, you will try to escape reality. Addictive substances, such as alcohol, drugs, or sweets, can temporarily give you the feeling that all is well. For other people, it may be that certain distractions, such as the media, shopping, or excessive hard work are necessary to give them relief for a time from the unrest that lives deep within them. But whatever is the kind of "flight" behavior, the result will be the same: you will eventually lose your grounding that should be your "here and now" connection to your emotions and your body.

To be properly grounded means that you experience a flow of giving and receiving that connects you with the Earth. The giving flow means that you express yourself on Earth in a way that manifests your unique soul energy in your daily activities so that you experience joy and fulfillment. The receiving flow means that you enjoy what life has to offer and that you say "Yes" to being fully present on Earth – *here* and *now*. Not being fully grounded means that the inspiration in your heart does not, or just barely, manifests on Earth, so you are not able to give earthly form to your creativity. The result is that you experience a lack of fulfillment in many areas of your life.

This sense of lack, from not being grounded, can make you feel like an outsider who does not belong on Earth. You may wonder: "What am I doing here and what is the sense of it all?", so feelings of alienation, loneliness, and sadness emerge. If the giving flow falters, there also results the inability to fully receive. If you cannot fully enjoy what the earthly reality has to offer you, you then experience a deep turning away from yourself that makes it impossible to truly receive.

## Facing your own pain

The key to healing the root chakra, and thus creating a stable grounding, is to face the pain within yourself with loving acceptance and awareness. This is certainly not easy to do, as it takes courage to look with full openness at your deepest emotions of fear and despair. However, not wanting to see and experience that emotional charge will eventually bring greater problems with it. You can be stuck for years in a relationship or work environment that fails to nurture and inspire you, or you can become addicted or depressed. But whatever happens, fleeing reality eventually causes more pain than confronting it. In facing the pain, you confirm who you are: a being who is greater than the pain and who has the courage and the strength to face the pain and to overcome it, *and this is a healing experience.*

Facing the pain is something you can do consciously; for example, through self-reflection or certain forms of therapy. However, you can be certain that life itself will also continually present you with situations that require you to go within and to ask yourself what inspires you deeply and motivates you. Life itself is directed toward growth and healing, and in nature, everything is directed toward self-development: an acorn instinctively wants to become an oak tree, and a tadpole a frog. Your inner nature wants similarly to evolve and flourish, and life wants to support you in doing that.

For a human being, this process is one of being consciously engaged on your path of development and daring to entrust yourself to the inner power of your own nature. This innate human desire is as strong a motivating force as the instinctive impulse of the tadpole that wants to become a frog or the acorn that wants to become an oak tree. There is a knowing in your soul as to who you really want to be on Earth. In the same way that a tadpole instinctively carries within itself the blueprint of its ideal future as a full-grown frog, so there also exists in your heart the instinctive knowledge about the full development and expression of your potential as a human being. And just as the tadpole encounters obstacles and problems in its development, so you also experience inner and outer obstacles and resistance in the development of your unique nature on Earth.

Humans are the only creatures on Earth that are challenged to *consciously change inner obstacles into creative forces*. The human being is capable of transforming emotional burdens with conscious awareness. In human consciousness, this fully aware transformation leads to self-knowledge, understanding, and compassion. Animals are also capable of self- healing on an emotional level and they instinctively make use of this healing power of nature. However, they cannot deliberately choose to turn toward, or to turn away from, their emotional pain in the way humans can.

Animals have unconscious healing forces, whereas humans can *develop* conscious healing power when they dare to say "Yes" to their inner pain. By saying "Yes", I do not mean that you just tolerate the pain. I mean that you stop resisting the pain and allow the emotional burden to fully manifest itself in your body and your feelings so you can accept it with full awareness.

An example may clarify this. Suppose that from an early age you had the feeling that you did not belong. Maybe you were sensitive and introverted, and you found it difficult to express yourself in communication with others, or maybe there was little understanding in your family environment. Whatever the cause, this feeling of not belonging was so painful that you tried to push it from your consciousness. It could be that you shut yourself off from your emotions and from your surroundings. Maybe you had a hobby or a fantasy world into which you could easily flee and become absorbed. When you became an adult, you found work in which you could perform well and into which you could become totally engrossed. Your performance resulted in approval from others, so that hard work became addictive and an easy way to not have to feel anything until you began to demand too much from your body and your mind, and you were eventually confronted with burnout.

When such a thing happens, you are faced with a choice: "Will I heal only the surface symptoms of the burnout or do I go deeply within and ask why I *need* to work so hard?" This is a time when you can choose to turn toward the deep pain of the child within you that feels emotionally abandoned. Saying "Yes" to this pain means that you allow the child within you to express what it is still feeling. You can, with your imagination, encourage this child to make known to you what it is experiencing. Perhaps you see the fear, sadness, or loneliness well up; especially the feelings that you were trying to mask by hard work. In saying "Yes" to the pain, you are also saying "Yes" to the child within you, and you ask it to be completely present in your life. In time, you will notice that this child not only carries with it negative emotions, but also quite *positive* emotions, such as cheerfulness, hope, and a sense of adventure. The child holds your blueprint: *the seed to growing into a fully mature oak tree.*

The blueprint of your soul is never lost. Time and time again it offers new opportunities to realize yourself. Sometimes a crisis, or a dead-end, are needed to get you to the point where you truly have to decide *for yourself,* and to choose *for your own nature*. There is *no wrong way* to come Home to who you are and it is also *never too late* to align with the blueprint of your soul. The soul is eternal and transcends living and dying in a mortal body. Rest assured that there *is* time and that there will always *be* new opportunities. Nevertheless, it is important to make a choice for yourself, so that you prevent the emotional pain from deepening and causing you to suffer needlessly. Turning away or fleeing from the accumulated pain in the root chakra holds you back from a fulfilling life on Earth. *It is my desire to see you thrive and manifest your potential here!* Just as a fully mature oak tree enriches itself and its environment, so will the manifestation of your soul energy enrich the Earth with valuable inspiration. My wish is to see you come to full maturity and I know that this wish corresponds to the blueprint of your soul. *You and I have a common goal.*

How do you restore the balance and harmony in your root chakra? How do you learn to trust the Earth again and to connect with the emotions and feelings that live within you? How do you create stable grounding in which the flow of giving and receiving abound?

## 1. Recognize the value and power of emotions

You do it by not repressing your emotions. Your emotions connect you with the inner child and the spontaneous, uncensored emotional life within you. This emotional life is the source from which comes your power and is the seat of your passion, your zeal, and your unique being. A young child considers itself to be the center of the world. It does not as yet experience reality from imposed standards and ideas. Only later does a mental filter obscure its perception of the world. Initially, the child does not doubt what it feels. If there is anything that is unsettling, it allows emotions such as anger, fear, and sadness to flow through as a natural power without restraint or judgement. The child can yet do no other.

As an adult, you can see this happen in a child and you realize that you have lost this innate spontaneity. How does this happen? In your adult world, people try to control their natural flow of emotions by managing and tempering them. Many of you are afraid of the power of emotions. This power is associated with chaos, impulsiveness, and irrationality. By wanting to restrain the flow of emotions through your fear, you make a negative judgment about your emotions. You drive a wedge between you and your feelings. For example, you feel anger arise within yourself and immediately you say inwardly: "This is not good". Or you feel fear and you immediately condemn it by thinking that fear is something that must be repressed, with the result that a conflict and split arises within you. Through the mistrust of your emotions, you turn against a natural strength in yourself that you need in order to live a life inspired by your soul.

Your emotions connect you with life itself. The natural force that manifests itself in emotions is not irrational, chaotic, or destructive. *Emotions are aimed precisely at restoring harmony*. An emotion that you accept consciously allows you to better understand yourself. In this way, an emotion such as anger or fear, embraced with awareness, helps you to understand in what ways you are sensitive and vulnerable. The conscious handling of emotions can deepen and strengthen your connection with yourself, and in this way, you bring harmony into your life. Only when you deny your emotions systematically and repress them, do they become explosive and uncontrollable over time. You cannot indefinitely deny that which lives deep within you. If you do, emotions will eventually manifest as a disruptive occurrence in your life. However, they can be likened to a rain storm. After awhile, the storm stops by itself and the sun begins to again shine. It is a natural phenomenon that has a beginning and an end. An emotion is like a wave that is best allowed to roll quietly onto the beach. If you want to dam it or obstruct it halfway, you create counter-currents that will eventually batter you.

The key to this process is that you begin to work together *with* your emotions. Connecting with your emotions means that you do not resist them, but that you surround them with an attention that is free of judgment. If you are angry or sad, observe this within yourself and feel how this mood affects your body and your thoughts. Through observation, you take a step backward and you realize that you are *not* your emotion. The emotion is like a child that wants to be heard and seen, and you are the guide for this child. You reassure it, and you let it know that it is safe to make itself known to you. You can do this in a concrete way whenever you feel emotional about something, and you do this by encouraging the emotion to make itself known in the form of a child. Let this child come toward you in your imagination and allow it to express itself freely and spontaneously. Give the child your attention and compassion, and tell it that you understand its feelings and that you receive the message it longs to give to you.

What do you do with this message? The choice is yours. Suppose you feel hurt and rejected by someone. You have consciously admitted to this emotional pain and have faced it. Now you ask yourself how you can best support the child within you. It may be that the pain is already largely resolved by your devotion to the child. Along with that, you can also feel the need to speak to the other person about what you have experienced. If there is an opening with that person, the encounter may deepen the relationship between you. However, it could also be that you feel there can be *no* opening with the other person and that you decide to seek less contact with that person and to focus on other contacts that nurture and inspire you. Connecting with your emotions means that you take their messages seriously and in consultation with the child within you, feel and weigh what feels best for you as a course of action. The key is that you cooperate with your emotions rather than fight them.

## 2 Experience the natural beauty in and around you

The first chakra, called the root chakra, represents your connection with the Earth. Finding a place in nature that you like and where you feel comfortable can help you to connect with me in a gentle and safe way. Every human being is sensitive to the beauty of nature: the trees, plants, and flowers; the animals, birds, and clouds; the course of the seasons. The simple rhythm and harmony of nature inspires awe, and you can be moved by the beauty and innocence of life in nature. Go regularly to a natural setting that evokes these feelings in you. If you cannot go outside, then look at the plants on your balcony or the flowers in a vase on your table. When you enjoy the beauty that you perceive, realize of what this beauty consists. This is not an idealized beauty. What you see does not meet society's predetermined norms and standards. It is a *wild* beauty that is not concerned with approval from others, and it is a beauty that evokes an inner sense of peace and harmony within you. You feel the surrender of the plants and trees as they silently submit to the seasons. You feel the innocence of the animals that gently and quietly follow the pace of their lives. A wisdom speaks through nature that brings you into connection with your own nature, your own inner knowing.

What I ask of you is that you see and recognize yourself *in* nature. Amidst the harmony and simplicity that you find there, you may feel left out as a human being: an outcast from paradise. You, however, are no outsider – *you are a part of nature*. The beauty, balance, and rhythm you observe in nature flows also through your being. Because of your excessively active thinking mind, it can be difficult to connect, within yourself, with this flow of tranquility and simplicity. But if you allow the beauty of nature to completely penetrate into you by coming in oneness with that feeling, you come Home to the non-thinking, silently knowing presence within yourself.

Your body is the bridge between you and nature. Through your body, you are connected with me. Look for a moment at your body in the same way that you look at the wildness of nature, and admire your body. You are accustomed to seeing your body in a judgmental way: is it attractive, strong, and healthy enough? These are *outer* standards, but can you also feel your body from within? Can you experience the primal power and the wisdom of your body? Can you feel how your body wants to be nurtured, and to be free to experience life in its own way, regardless of exterior standards that have been imposed upon you? The prevailing standards of beauty and health create a yoke under which you suffer in trying to live up to them. Your society designs images of beauty and health that are inauthentic and contrived, and as cold and clinical as the minds that conceived them. These images find no basis in reality; they are not bearers of truth. Look at the diversity of living beings in nature; even the petals on a flower are all different and unique. No single being in nature strives to resemble another. The obligation of each living creature is to be itself, because when everything is themselves, there is then harmony in the whole.

That is also what you experience in the natural wilderness as "beauty": you experience the harmony of all things being a part of the whole. Everything and everyone has its own place and contributes by being itself in coherence with the whole, and you, too, are a part of that whole. You have a unique contribution to make, simply by being who you are. How do you know who you are? You experience this by fully letting go of outer norms and standards. What is your deepest desire? What are the dreams of your heart? Can you make space in your daily life for what you really desire? Do you dare break away from what is inauthentic and contrived in your life? Follow your own nature and you will find your place within the whole. Trust that your own wild nature produces the same harmonious beauty as nature's wildness. You are accustomed to adjusting to the demands and expectations of society, but what the Earth and humanity really need now are leaders, not followers. We need people who dare to connect with their deepest nature; with the most original, lively, warm parts of themselves and with what makes them grounded and inspired human beings.

## 3. Connect with your body

Focus your attention for a moment entirely on your body. Imagine that you are a part of nature, such as a strong, big tree is a part of nature. Inside you flow energies and fluids that know exactly where they have to be. Your heart is beating, your blood is flowing, and all organs, tissues, and cells in your body strive naturally toward health and vitality. Feel that you are included in the healing and renewing force that is essential to nature. Your body has a self-healing capability and you can connect with that capability simply by listening to its messages. Your body may tell you that you need rest, relaxation, and enjoyment, or attention and being held by another.

Your body not only tells you about the physical aspects of yourself, it also tells you about your emotional well-being. Your body is closely connected with your emotions. Listening to the signals from your body is nourishing for your soul. Your body is a finely tuned instrument that should be considered as a messenger of your soul, which reveals itself in and through your body. Your body is not something "lower" that must be transcended, it is a gift that can bring you into a deeper connection with who you are in your essence. You are accustomed to seeing your body from the outside and assessing it. Feel it now from within, and feel the Earth force that is alive in it. Feel the presence of your soul that has entered into a dance with your body.

Imagine there is a warm life force in your root chakra. At the top of your tailbone is the sacrum, the sacred bone, where you can perceive or visualize a glowing red globe. From this inner fire, allow a healing energy to flow throughout your entire body – through your legs and feet, your spine, your abdomen. Let this energy flow up to your shoulders, your arms, your hands, while, at the same time, it flows down into your feet – *feel this flow from within*. Become conscious of the life in all the parts of your body. Now ask your body: "How do you feel? Is there anything I can do for you? Do you need something from me?" Ask and wait quietly and patiently. It may be that your body does not respond immediately, so perhaps you need to get used to talking with your body – and you can learn to do that. Your body responds to your attention – *it basks in it!* You are its inspiration and the sun in its universe. You can positively influence your body by enveloping it with your consciousness, and by saying "Yes" to the dance that you have undertaken with it.

Your soul manifests itself in and through your body. Connect with your root chakra to see if there is doubt or fear there that inhibits you from being completely present in your body and on the Earth. Embrace the doubt or fear with love and compassion. Do not condemn it; allow it to be, but stay present with the pain. By remaining present with the pain, you dissolve it. Contrary to what you often think, you do not have to "work on yourself". The aim is to remain present whenever pain and fear reveal themselves in your emotional life and to not run away from them. By just being there for yourself – in all openness and acceptance – the pain is transformed into strength. By embracing your fear and pain, you transform them and thereby you feel safe and secure on Earth. Only you can give this safety and security to yourself. Real safety and security do not exist because the world welcomes and affirms you – *that you do for yourself.*

Cooperate with your emotions. Recognize the beauty of nature in you and make the connection with your body through the above ways of healing your root chakra. Using these approaches to your body, you create a channel for your soul to deeply connect with the Earth. When your soul is immersed in your everyday earthly being, you experience joy, abundance, and fulfillment. This is your destiny as a human being and not a distant dream – *it is a real possibility*. Just as the acorn naturally grows into an oak tree, and the tadpole into a frog, so are you intended to radiate as a human Angel on Earth.

## Journey through the elements

I am the voice of Earth. I speak to you from the ground beneath your feet. I bear you continuously, as well as being present in your body. The body in which you dwell enables you to experience life here. I represent Home, just as much as does heaven. I am a primal force wanting to provide you with a sense of security, in which you can relax and be free. Being Home essentially means feeling free to be who you are. Being yourself is something simple and yet incredibly diverse. You all long to be yourself and you all long to be free from worry, fear, and sorrow, so make the connection with me. I wish to nurture you and to receive and support you – *we are one*. I am present inside you through your body, and your body continually sends messages to you about your life's path.

Let us go on a journey with your body, and travel through the basic elements of nature: water, fire, air, and earth. These elements represent the life energies that together weave the web of Creation. Follow me, and see this as a game – keep it light-hearted and playful.

## Water: element of surrender

Imagine you are in nature. You stand with your bare feet on the ground on the shore of a lake and you are nude. There is no one there, just you, and you feel free. You are not ashamed of being nude; it feels natural and comfortable. You feel the ground beneath your feet and then you move some steps forward and feel the water wash over them. The water is warm and soothing, and it calms you. You feel no resistance – it is delightful. You go deeper and deeper into the lake and you sense the healing power of the water – it is from a pure source. It helps you to let go of what you no longer need. Now float on your back in this lake and feel the element of water around you.

Feel as if the water washes through your body and through your blood, which itself contains the element of water. Water is in and around you – you hear its

73

reassuring sound – and you let it cleanse you. Sense within your body to discover if there is something in particular you want to let go of. Do not ponder whether it is possible to do so; just feel the longing to be free of it. It may be a situation in your life that is difficult or an emotion that bothers you. Name it and surrender it to the water. You do not need to know how this will happen; just say to yourself: "I release this. May the water rinse it from me and cleanse me." The water brings flow and change, so surrender yourself to this flow.

## Fire: element of inspiration

As you gently float back to the shore, you see the Sun shining above you as a ball of fire in the sky. You leave the water and lie down on the shore so the Sun can dry you with its warm and nurturing rays. As you feel your body basking in the sunlight, you feel the energy of the Sun and you connect with it. Feel the Sun's essence flow through you in a gentle and tender way.

There is a place in your body connected to the power of the Sun. It is your solar plexus, the area of your third chakra located near your stomach. Feel a warm, relaxed flow in that center and ask yourself: "What is it I would like to create in my life – what is it that inspires me?"

You do not need to find the words for it, just let the feeling be there. Within you is an inner desire to manifest your unique quality on Earth – *your love*. Let the sunlight make you aware of that inspiration: it is your inner fire, warm and full of life. Let the energy of the Sun also pour into your throat. Your throat is the energy center for self expression, your showing yourself to the outside world with trust and self-worth.

# Air: element of the mind

You sit quietly on the shore of the lake and feel how the elements of water and fire assist you on your inner journey. You then notice a soft breeze on your cheeks. It is the air, the element of spaciousness and openness, which is, at the same time, secure and playful. With it, you can play securely within the grand cosmos that surrounds you. Feel the air come into your body through the breath. Breathe in and feel the breath flow down into your abdomen – then breathe out. Air brings in spaciousness in which to play and move. Air is the most cosmic among the elements and brings inspiration to you from your soul. You feel as light as the air, because air does not take any solid form. Allow yourself to dare to fly and be free. You are not truly bound to your body or to any form. The element of air reminds you of this – *you are free as a bird.*

# Earth: element of form

Now again feel how you are sitting on the ground at the shore of the lake and connect to the element of earth. Sense the firmness of the ground beneath you and notice the fertility of the Earth that shows itself in the many plants, flowers, and trees surrounding you. Feel the maternal power in me – I am a female energy. I flow through all your body and you can clearly sense me in your tail bone, the first or root chakra at the base of your spine. Sense that a cord connects your root chakra to the heart of the Earth. Note the flexibility of this cord – it is not a cord that binds or restricts you. It is a cord that enables you to be here on the Earth and to joyfully express your deepest inspiration.

# Choose an element to work with

Know that the four elements are available to you. They flow inside you, as well as all around you. You are Home here – you belong to the Earth and all the elements. You are creators and you are meant to be a master of the elements. They want to serve you.

We have spoken about the difference between the dimension of nature and that of the human world. Many of you feel stuck in the confines of human society. The hurry and agitation, often present there, dictate an unnatural rhythm that unsettles you. Do not be frightened of this; you are strong enough to deal with it. Do, however, dig your roots deep into the realm of nature. Play with the elements, for therein lies your Home. It is the energy of natural living that your soul wants to contribute to society at this time. The spiritual transformation now occurring in humanity is about a return to the Earth, to a way of living in which your life flow is aligned with nature, both outside you and inside you.

In human society, much emphasis has been placed on thinking and controlling life. Many of you try to bring structure to your life from conditioned notions that come from the head rather than from the heart. If you do so, you are oblivious to the great Powers, both earthly and cosmic, that shape your life. You plan, and you try to control life from your head, and when life runs counter to your expectations, you interpret this as adversity and ill fate. The art of natural living is to let go of so much thinking and controlling. There has been an excess of that in your society. This new time encourages you to now align yourself with the natural rhythm and flow of Earth.

I am your Home, so allow me to nurture you. Let the elements in your body speak. Ask them what you need and it will be given to you. I hear your heartbeat and want to help you find your way. Now hear my heartbeat, too. You bring inspiration and cosmic light to me. I absorb what you give and I am grateful for your presence. Restore your unity with me.

# Communicating with animals

It fills me with joy to be present in your midst and to be welcomed by you. You see me, Mother Earth, as a full partner in Creation, and you welcome me because you value my beauty. You are concerned with nature and feel a connection with the animal kingdom, so you are open to a connection with me. I thank you for being open, because a connection between us is something that can benefit us both very much.

Ultimately, we are one. We are born of one consciousness, the consciousness of God, who manifests in many ways and takes on many forms of experience. One consciousness flows through us all: through the human, animal, plant, and mineral kingdoms. Feel at this moment the unity that makes it possible that we, in our diversity, can communicate with one another, can learn from one another, and can enrich one another's lives. This is the purpose of our lives being woven together: that you feel enriched by all that lives on Earth, especially by the animals that surround you as loyal companions.

Anyone who feels attracted to this subject has experienced a deep connection with animals, now or in the past. This connection extends beyond the taking care of an animal – something moved in your heart and was stirred emotionally. When this inner stirring happened, you gave something worthwhile to the animal kingdom. By your attention and openness to an animal in your life, you gave an important energy to the animal kingdom.

Animals desire to be acknowledged and appreciated by humans and valued for what they are: a part of Creation. When you treat animals with respect and caring, they become happy. You sometimes worry if you are doing enough to alleviate the suffering of animals. You observe how animals are treated disrespectfully and this knowledge affects you with a heavy and despondent feeling, and some of you even become depressed as a result.

I want to tell you something about the spiritual significance of the animal kingdom, and about the possibility of a joyful cooperation between humans and animals. I want you to understand clearly about your role relative to animals: what you can do for them and what you can receive from them.

## The connection between humans and animals

All life forms on Earth have a purpose. Everything that lives is in the process of progression and development – is in a creative dance. However, humans have free will and this distinguishes them from all other living beings on Earth. With this free will, humans can shape reality in a way that is not possible for animals. Animals live from a natural, inborn instinct. Energetically, they are strongly linked with their own kind and live mainly from their essence as a specie. Their individuality is not yet as strongly awakened as it is in humans. Humans possess individuality and from that give form to their lives. You use your mental and will powers to manifest your ideas into a material reality.

The freedom to create is, on the one hand, a gift to humans and a source of their power, while on the other hand, this ability can also lead to imbalance, violence, and destruction. When you live too much from your thinking and willing, and you want too much to direct and organize and manipulate, you lose connection with the totality to which you belong. You no longer experience the natural bond with other living beings and you find yourself feeling separate and lonely.

As history shows, humans try to assert their might over nature and want to subject it into subservience. This impulse has a destructive impact on nature – on the animals, plants, and minerals – and you also suffer because of that impulse. You become estranged from your own nature, your spontaneity, and your feelings. No other living creature on Earth can feel as lonely and lost as do humans. Animals instinctively feel a connection with the whole and this feeling is natural for them. They do not doubt their connection and therefore surrender easily to life. Animals live in the *now* and do not think about the future.

Sadly, humans have lost their natural connection with life. Self-awareness, and the creative power of humans, constitute not only a source of power and a gift;

they also have been a trap into which humanity has obviously fallen. However, this does not take away from the fact that you also carry a promise within you to enrich all living creatures on Earth. On a subconscious level, the animal kingdom knows of this promise, so in the animal kingdom there is still respect for humanity and the promise that lies at the hearts of humans.

What is this promise that is the spiritual aim of the journey that humans are taking on Earth? It is the willingness to use your creative consciousness in cooperation with nature from a mutual giving and receiving, so that life on Earth can fully develop into an innovative dance of Creation. Nature can provide for your needs and can inspire you by her beauty, balance, and harmony, and you can give something to nature in return. Nature also gives to you an opportunity for growth in consciousness whenever you connect with her with respect and openness. I would like to explain this process in more detail.

## The birth of individuality in animals

Consciousness is present in everything that is alive on Earth, even in plants and minerals. Animals are the most identifiable to humans as conscious, sentient beings because they are the most individuated beings present in nature. You can see an animal move purposefully, deliberately, and in response to its environment. The consciousness in plants and minerals is naturally more passive and dreamier, and is therefore less visible, which is why it is easier for you to connect with animals than with other forms of life on Earth.

When you approach an animal with loving attention, you help that animal to realize that it is unique; that it is a particular individual with its own experience, its own inner world, and that it is not just one of its kind. In this way, humans contribute to the growth of individuated consciousness in animals: they feel their consciousness grow when they are connected to humans. When you connect with an animal with your attention and love, the animal awakens to itself This happens very clearly in your relationship with your pets, because you develop a unique bond with these animals.

79

By receiving your human consciousness, an animal becomes acquainted with different experiences than those it knows only through its animal nature. It is open to this experience because it wants to explore more deeply the entire range of feeling and living. And this kind of connection with humans has a broad effect on the entire animal kingdom. Your connection with a particular animal not only increases its self-awareness, the connection also increases the self-awareness of the entire species of which that animal is a part.

Pets often pick up on the emotions of their owners, even though they may be negative emotions. It is something that animals chose from their souls: they wanted to learn something from the kinds of awareness and emotions that people emit. Sometimes it can tax an animal to sense the moods of its owner, which can even cause physical complaints and behavioral problems in the animal. Yet animals take this as part of their compact with humans. They want to be with you from a desire to come into greater consciousness and also *because they love you.* As many of you know, pets show an incredible loyalty and willingness to serve humans. The attention and love that you give to them, they return doubly.

Spiritually, the connection with animals can also be very helpful for you. Through their presence, animals can stimulate you to open up emotionally and to come out of your head and to trust life. Animals can bring to you grounding, relaxation, and peace. The pure love of an animal can make you realize that *you are loved*, regardless of how you perform or how you look. Animals can bring you back to your essential nature. From an energetic point of view, a beautiful interaction takes place between humans and animals. You stimulate the birth of individuality in animals, and animals stimulate in you a feeling of belonging.

What animals want, and where all life on Earth is moving toward, is growth in consciousness: *self-awareness and the formation of free will and individual expression.* With the birth of self-awareness arises individuality, and with individuality arises true creativity. When you are an individual – a conscious, creative being – you can act outside the laws of nature and create something new, and that can happen only if you are able to depart from learned habits and innate instincts. The birth of individuality in a living being is something truly important on its path of development – *it is the equivalent of the birth of the soul.*

Animals are living beings who are in the process of being born as an individual soul through a long process of inner development. Humans have an individual soul already and, in fact, are so advanced that you have even experienced the excesses and pitfalls of a too strongly developed free will. People can help animals to self-awareness, and animals can help people feel at home on Earth by bringing them back to their connectedness with nature.

## Alleviating animal suffering

I want to also comment on the question of how you can alleviate the suffering of animals. Many of you are touched in your hearts by the disrespectful treatment of animals in the world. Some of you have become disturbed by and feel a heavy burden of pain and sadness and powerlessness when confronted with this suffering. I want to give a few suggestions to you by which the relating to, and assisting of animals, can become a joyful cooperation in which you both become inspired.

*Realize that your consciousness is creative.*

Realize that in your deepest essence and nature you are a healer, a caretaker for the Earth. From your soul, you are deeply connected to me because there is an ancient agreement between us. You wanted to incarnate as a soul to enrich me, Earth, with your loving consciousness. You also wanted to come here to enjoy your connectedness with the wealth of life and its experience as it manifests on Earth. By being here, by appreciating the beauty and the harmony in nature, and by emanating your natural radiance wherever you go, you already help to bring healing to the animals on Earth.

You may, perhaps, doubt whether this is enough, but realize that consciousness is always creative. When you can hold, on Earth, to a consciousness that is imbued with the love of nature and with warmth and respect for animals, then this consciousness is felt and observed by animals and by me. It is natural for people to ask themselves whether they are doing enough, and then to look for concrete, visible opportunities to do more. However, it is through the radiance of your consciousness that things harmonize and change without you doing or saying anything.

*Honor the way of animals*

Realize that animals have their own consciousness. They have chosen their life on Earth – to learn and to grow in consciousness here. Animals are inwardly prepared to give much and to be of service to humans, although it is certainly true that they suffer from disrespectful treatment. However, it does not help them if you see them as victims and react to their pain and suffering. *Honor their way!* It helps them most if you remain yourself and then discover how you can contribute positively to their well-being. Animals are happy with little and need only the generosity of a small gesture.

*Keep the balance between giving and receiving*

Attune yourself inwardly to the animal, or the animals, which you want to help. Sense what is possible, what feels joyful for you, and by what you are inspired – this is your path for healing animals. Remember, you are here to give form to your own unique soul's light. Do what your feelings tell you to do and what brings you joy. Allow yourself to be inspired from within – follow the flow of your heart. Also, when it comes to wanting to make a change in consciousness that will benefit animals, there is a natural rhythm and timing that you cannot force.

Helping animals needs to be something joyful, in which you give and receive, and which is *mutually* inspired toward growth in awareness. From your urge to eliminate suffering, it is possible that you will give *too* much and lose sight of your own boundary, while animals have their own well developed sense of boundary. To find out whether you are trying to give too much, you can inwardly consult an animal and ask what it wants from you. This is often something other than what you expect. You can also ask for an inner guide in the form of an animal. Allow an animal to enter your imagination and ask the animal for a message. Look at your dealings with animals as a two-way street. See yourself as receiver, as well as giver.

*Trust your gut*

When making intuitive connections with animals, you can come up against much self-doubt: "Am I sensing this connection correctly, or is it all in my head? Is what I imagine not a projection on my part?" See this process of making connection with animals as a journey where you are asked to let go of your head and to set sail by the compass of your feelings. When you do find yourself being hampered by your thinking, make no judgments about this – *all humans live too much in their heads!*

You feel attracted to communicating with animals because you want to let go of the overly mental and to open more deeply to the intuitive and to feelings, and, in this way, to come closer to your inner knowing. So, when you notice that you are in doubt, that you are unsure about your ability to communicate with animals, then see this as an opportunity to notice the fear in yourself and to encourage yourself to let that go. Animals are happy to help you do that. In their eyes, you are quickly forgiven for your mistakes. They feel the sincerity of your intention, and that means a lot to them.

Feel for a moment the presence of the animals with whom you have connected in one way or another, both those living and those that have passed on. Animals who have died also stay connected with you; their loyalty is deep and stretches across multiple lives and defies centuries. Feel their presence – they are gathered here around you. Let them tell you where they are and what would make them happy to receive from you. They speak not only for themselves, but also for the greater whole of the animal kingdom.

For a moment, feel and see how excited they are. Yes, some of them carry emotional wounds, and yet ... *look how much joy there is in them!* They feel honored by the connection that you make with them, to be acknowledged and accepted by you. Open up to what they want to give to you. Feel how in their own simple way they encourage you to just be yourself: to feel what you feel, to be who you are, to believe in yourself – just uncomplicated and in the *now*.

See the power and full health of these animals. Feel their zest for life and their strength, their faith, their service, and their love – *enjoy their positive energy!* Answer their call for cooperation with them as equal partners in the adventure of earthly creation.

## The healing power of nature

Enjoy the Spring, when life unfolds in a new round of growth and blossoming. Allow yourself to be delighted by the colors and the shapes that you see, the fresh sounds that you hear, the calming power of new life. You are a part of nature and you are also included in the cycle of the seasons. In you, the new Spring also comes to life.

Many of you have difficulty being here on Earth. When you look around, you often experience this world as a dark and dreary place where reigns violence and oppression toward people and nature. Feeling this can make you gloomy and sad. Many of you have been born with resistance in your body, with a sense of: "Do I have to re-incarnate on Earth, in this setting of pain, fear, and sluggishness?" There lives in you a nostalgia for a reality where harmony, gentleness, and joy prevail. In your heart, you remember this feeling, this energy, and when you are in the freedom of nature, this memory in your soul again awakens.

In the freedom of nature, you reawaken to the beauty, the harmony, and the connection which you carry in your heart. It is what you so long for, and nature can bring you Home to who you really are. The silence, the rhythm, the rest you can experience there reflects deeply who you are. In nature, you can experience a regaining of your balance, yet at the same time this experience evokes homesickness and sadness. There lives in you a deep desire for a reality that is free of the heavy, negative energies on Earth. The question is: how do you deal with this sadness and this desire?

It is important for you to realize that these feelings are not wrong. Homesickness is the call of your soul: a remembrance to help you to recall *who you are in your essence*. Your soul *wanted* to incarnate on Earth. From a very deep place within you, you have chosen to be here, even though there are parts of you that occasionally lose courage and resist. By connecting with your soul, you remember not only who you are, you also remember that you are here for a purpose. The homesickness you feel refers not only to a lack, a deficiency, but also to a positive purpose – *that you are here to manifest harmony and unity.*

How do you do this? How do you bring this purpose and its energy into everyday life? *The key lies in reminding yourself of who you are in everything you do.* The more you hear the voice of your soul in your daily pursuits, the more you align with your life's purpose. I would like to tell you how nature can help you to remember your true self. In particular, I will focus on the healing power of plants and trees.

All the trees and plants, with their flowers, that live on Earth are rooted in the energetic flow of unity that supports life. In other words, the plant kingdom is very close to God, to the Source, or whatever you call this divine flow of energy and consciousness. Consciousness in plants and trees is barely, or not at all, individuated, such as is the case in humans, and to some extent in animals. Through the plant kingdom flow universal energies that are connected to the angelic realm. Trees and plants have no such thing as an ego, an individual "I" that stands and acts in the world. The consciousness of the plant kingdom has an unbroken connection with the whole. Trees and plants are direct manifestations of the realm of the angels.

Angels are a part of the vibrant, energy fields that radiate unity and love. While the divine manifests itself in humans as individual souls, in the angelic realm the divine takes the form of trans-personal, universal energy fields. There are different energy fields in the angelic realm, all of which emanate a specific quality, such as love, or courage, or clarity. The plant kingdom on Earth developed its material forms by utilizing the energy of angels that are oriented toward unity and harmony. You experience this feeling in an almost self-evident way when you are in nature and become calm and return to yourself. By being open to nature, you receive the healing power of the angelic realm – yet there is more. Whenever you align yourself with this angelic energy, you realize that in your essence, you are one with this energy; in other words, *that you are an angel.*

# Your origin as an angel

You have not always been human. Before you incarnated on Earth as a human being and began your long cycle of lives, you were an angel. You were in a less dense plane of existence – a more ethereal setting than you experience now as a human. You had yet no earthly body and you were not constrained by the laws of time and space. You could go and be where you chose. The creative power of your thoughts enabled you to immediately manifest what you desired. There was still no I-awareness in you as you now know it. You felt strongly linked with a group of angels: the vibrant energy field to which you belonged. You experienced yourself as a part of a larger organism.

Imagine that you are an angel and that you are not yet bound to a human body. Maybe you see yourself as a sphere of light, or as a literal figure of an angel with wings. It does not matter how you visualize this angel, it is, above all, about feeling the lightness and freedom that correspond to this awareness. From this plane, you chose to become involved in the creative adventure on Earth. Know that angels themselves are also in development, because nothing in the universe is static. You were creative, enterprising angels, who felt attracted to planet Earth and saw that here, a multitude of life forms could emerge with opportunities for their growth of consciousness. You wanted to test your own power to create, as well as to support the Earth in her development and to inspire her. As an angel, those qualities of life renewal and adventurousness belonged to your angelic energy field.

Imagine that you, as an angel, implanted thought forms as "seeds" into the consciousness of plants on Earth, causing all sorts of new forms to arise: new plant species, a refinement of existing species, beautiful flowers – a true diversity of life forms. Imagine how the image of a beautiful flower arose spontaneously in your mind and how you fondly offered this image to a plant that you felt was receptive. Out of your ethereal body flowed the power of your imagination into nature, into the plants and the minerals. These earthly beings received your ethereal seed-thoughts that gradually began to manifest within their physical forms. In this way, you helped to develop life on Earth.

Maybe this all sounds fanciful and far-fetched, and too much like a fairytale for your modern minds. Nevertheless, I ask you to let it play in your imagination and to feel whether you recognize something in it. Feel the love in your heart for life on Earth and how deeply you are bonded with me. You have been a co-creator with me of the life forms here. I myself am an angelic being, a nature spirit or deva who worked with you in ancient times – in joy and gaiety. I was already embodied in matter as a planet, and I was the receptive soil that received your creative energy.

My angel quality is harmony. The energy field that I radiate as an angel helps to make possible the peaceful coexistence of different life forms. I want everything that lives on me to feel and be connected. I want to reveal the unity that exists throughout all diversity. Once people recognize how they are interconnected with other people, and with everything that lives on Earth, harmony and peaceful coexistence will be possible. This is my dream, my vision.

As an angel, you contributed to the fulfillment of my dream. From a desire for unity and inspiration, you connected with life on Earth; but later, when you incarnated as humans, you forgot this. You came to know the reality of the body and the cycle of birth and death. You began to experience the duality of light and dark, love and fear. And as you descended more deeply into matter, you began to lose your connection to the angelic realm and with the angel that you are. However, this happened for a reason – this was not a mistake or an error. There are intentions behind your journey of incarnation. One of the intentions is that you allow your angel light to descend deeply into matter, so it becomes visible in my physical reality.

## Feeling at home on Earth

I know it sometimes seems impossible for you to hold on to your light in this physical reality. There are times when you wonder whether you belong here, or if you are even welcome here. You experience fear, doubt, and uncertainty when you try to manifest and express who you truly are. These feelings stem from memories of rejection, which come from this life or from previous lives. The pain that you experienced then has not left you.

Some of you have sworn never again to give of yourself when on Earth. You have decided to swallow your passion and your dreams and desires in order to never again be so vulnerable. I understand how this happened; however, this hardening comes with a price. By not wanting to again give of yourself, you disconnect from your soul and you reduce your consciousness to the level of the persons by whom you were rejected. By pulling back, you admit defeat, and mistrust and cynicism triumph over openness and optimism. In your heart then is a sadness, because your soul continues to desire to fulfill its destiny: *to become a fully incarnated angel on Earth.*

In order to feel at home on Earth, and to open your heart again to life here, it helps to make connection with the angel energy that you sense in nature. When you are in nature and you perceive the harmony around you, you feel your original connection with me. Your bond with me is older than your being human, and this bond does not have to be undermined by the fear and rejection you have experienced in human society. There is a great difference between my feeling and energy, and that of human society. You can experience this difference especially in quiet places in nature. Here you can experience that the spiritual Home for which you long is not located somewhere in an other-worldly or heavenly plane. Home is not far away – it is *here*, just below your feet. My original energy of harmony and unity is familiar to you; I embody the energy of Home for you.

Feel again who you are – recognize your own beauty, grace, and divine inspiration. You do not have to remember this literally, from your human memory, but feel the truth in your being. The gentleness, beauty, and harmony that you experience in nature is the energy of Home, the energy of your origin – *the energy of your soul.* That is why it affects you so deeply when you see how nature is being violated by people, and that is why it fills you with reverence to be in nature with the plants, the animals, and in the open air in the woods or by the sea.

Try not to judge what people are doing with nature – focus on *your* life. Do what makes your heart sing, and in this way you naturally carry the energy and feeling of harmony on Earth. You let your light shine the strongest when you feel at Home here on Earth. If you remember who you are, the old pain that you carry within you will no longer block you. Remembering who you are opens your heart – *you become inspired*. When you dare to live in openness from your soul; your true beauty is visible to others. And when you are open to life – straight through to the old pain – it transforms that pain into a bridge to the heart of another.

Meet me, angel to angel. You are an angel and I am one, too. I know you and you know me. I am still the receptive ground upon which your soul can play and dance. *You are welcome!* As an Angel you came to me with your energy of renewal and adventure, and you descended into my physical reality. On this path of descent, you sometimes get confused, but do not let that discourage you. I can still see who you are. Trust and live again according to your deepest desires and your boldest dreams.

## The dance between man and woman

I am Earth, and my soul is connected to your soul. I am present in your body, your being, your nature, and I am the ground on which you stand as human beings. Together we journey on the path to a new era in which unity and connection will be slowly restored. The potential already exists for a world in which the pain, fear, and sadness of the past are processed and released. You can make a contribution to this new world, and you are needed to do so, because you are an active player in this process. How do you help make it happen? By being prepared to face your own pain, fear, and doubt – by entering bravely within yourself and taking a sincere look at what exists inside you – by taking pity on your pain – by not accusing the other person for what you feel – by discovering your own strength.

You have the power to heal yourself; your wholeness cannot be taken away by anyone. You hold the key to your own healing because *you are the creator of your own experiences*. When you realize this, it changes your relationship with everything outside you: the world, the people, and the situations you encounter. You become more independent, yet at the same time, you can now really connect with others, because you know who you are and you can remain yourself, no matter what happens.

A utopian fantasy? Not at all – this is to where you are going. This is to where the path of inner growth leads: to a powerful self-awareness that allows you to connect deeply with other persons and the world around you while you stay completely true to yourself, to your nature, and to your limitations. You come Home to who you really are: a unique soul, yet an integral part of the whole. You are a part of Creation, one with everything that lives and, simultaneously, you are an individual, unique and original. There is a place in your heart where you can experience your deepest essence and, at the same time, feel that you are connected to all life around you. To find this place in your heart is the purpose of your journey on Earth – to become *a carrier of light who helps to construct a new reality*.

# The role play of man and woman

It seems sometimes that the society in which you live is doing everything it can to keep you away from this place in your heart. You are taught from a young age that you are not one with others and that who you are is determined by the roles that you play. You are a girl or a boy, a child or a parent; you are a pupil or a teacher, employee or boss, rich or poor, beautiful or ugly. Because you identify with a certain role that you are playing, the connection with who you are in your essence becomes lost. You become alienated from yourself, and your relationships with others become empty and more superficial. If you are playing a role, you will not experience a true connection from heart to heart.

In this message, we will look especially at the roles you play as a man or a woman. These roles are largely determined by the history in which you find yourself. The traditions that formed your parents and grandparents still have their influence on you, and often these traditions were restrictive in their thinking and their application. What it meant to be a man or a woman was defined and determined by strict rules and standards. This meant that the worlds of men and women were artificially separated, but it is not my purpose here to discuss this history in detail. I ask you to now connect intuitively with the pain that originated in these traditions of alienation and the struggle between men and women that resulted, because you are a part of this history. Both sexes, both men and women, have suffered from the restrictions that were imposed upon them.

The female energy has been undervalued for a long time. In many cultures the female was, and still is, openly scorned and even suppressed in a violent way, while the male was regarded as superior. Thought processes, in the sense of the mental ordering of life, were considered of paramount importance, while feelings were held in disregard. However, when mental processes are not inspired by feeling and intuition, they become cold and oppressive. The result is a rigid form of thinking that has little regard for the playful, emotional, and creative aspects of life. This excessively mental male energy also held religion captive for a very long time. Discipline and coercion were considered necessary to maintaining control, so the female energy was oppressed, and not only in the hearts of women, but also in the hearts of men.

Every human being possesses both energies. As a soul, both the male and the female energies are parts of you. When men are forced to repress their emotions, there arises an idealized stereotype of what it is to be a man: an emotionally underdeveloped man who manifests mainly through thinking and action. This image is increasingly regarded as normal in your culture, where male leadership is associated with a dominant, hierarchical, power-oriented style of thinking and acting. In these qualities, the flowing and connecting aspects of the female energy are entirely absent. Under such a stereotype of masculinity, both men and women suffer. The oppression of the female energy has deeply affected both men and women in their humanness. I would now like to show how both men and women are each in their own way injured by this past and how you can release these restrictive roles.

## The female and the male wound

In the soul of women, the injury is visible as a deep feeling of inferiority and insecurity. As a result of the aggressive oppression of the female energy, women are usually no longer aware of their own strength. They view themselves as subordinate, often without being aware of this. Femininity has become associated with serving others: being nice, sweet, giving, and caring. This is the way in which the female role has become defined, and this is just as much a stereotype as is the emotionally crippled, dominant male role. No woman can be *only* that way without denying herself. Still, this was the idealized image that has been held for women for centuries.

The feeling of inferiority that has been imparted to women has meant that women find it difficult to embrace their true strength and to manifest it. However, once women embrace their strength, they will, at first, be portrayed as imitating men. That is the response that results when there is a break with traditional stereotypes. However, the idea is not that women become like men, but that the masculine and the feminine flow through women in a balanced way. This means that women honor their female energy and dare to live from passion and feeling, as well as dare to take care of themselves and to clearly establish their borders. To recover from the wound inflicted on the female energy, it is important that women become self-conscious and strong.

The male soul has also been wounded. Men have for centuries lost the connection with their own feelings as a result of the prevailing male dominance. The connection with their heart, with their emotions, and with the loving, caring aspects within themselves, has been seriously repressed. Masculinity has been associated with being tough and hard, which is at odds with feeling empathy toward others and with sharing one's feelings. Many men find it frightening to surrender to their feelings; doing so feels strange, awkward, and unsafe. However, men are suffering because of their lack of female energy and so they need to restore the connection with their souls.

The essential issue for women is that they regain their strength, their male side, and for men, that they dare to surrender to their feelings, to their female side. How this issue manifests itself in the everyday life of men and women will differ from individual to individual. In each human being, the female and male energies flow differently. For example, it is possible that you as a woman already have sufficient male energy and that you now need to learn to connect with your feelings. Or that you as a sensitive man feel at ease with the female energy, but that you find it difficult to set clear boundaries for yourself. The wounds of both sexes can manifest in both men and women. However, you can see that men in this new time on Earth are encouraged to connect with their feelings, their female side, while women are challenged to honor their own male energy and to use it, so they can powerfully and independently let their light shine across the world.

## Building the bridge to each other

Because both men and women have had a stereotyped image from the past forced upon them, they have come to view one another as almost of another specie, and as a result have become alienated from one another. This has caused a lot of misunderstanding and suffering for both women and men. Yet when masculinity and femininity are allowed to flow freely again within *both* men and women, there can be beautiful, deepening relationships between the two sexes.

At this time of history, the stereotyped and violent images of the past are faltering: women have been given more freedom and men may show more feeling. The traces of the past are far from erased, because the wounds are deep and heal slowly; yet even so, there is a change taking place. In the hearts of both women and men is a growing and perceptible desire for a real connection with each other. Many of you are becoming open to a loving relationship between a man and a woman in which you truly accept each other and give each other their freedom. Only then can you experience the unity that connects you with another and is the source of all life.

In each of you lives a desire for Home. There is a longing in your hearts that manifests as the feeling that "something is missing from my life". This "something" that you are missing is your natural connection with the whole. To be included in the whole, and to feel one with another, is what will make you truly happy. This connection gives meaning to life, and this is the path you are on in this new time.

Loving relationships between women and men are an essential part of your destiny. In these relationships, the desire for unity and connection emerges strongly. A romantic attraction can seize you fully, because in that attraction, the desire for unity and connection awakens at all levels: physical, emotional, and spiritual. Infatuation contains a promise that you will be able to give form to unity and connectedness in your everyday life. But to make that promise come true, more is needed than just infatuation.

You have a particular past as a man or as a woman that affects and influences your everyday life. You carry within yourself painful memories from the past which have caused you to establish judgments about life of which you may not even be aware. All this "baggage" that you carry can drive a wedge between you and your beloved, without you having a clear understanding of how and what exactly is happening. The pain that you experience when you become separated from your partner, through fear or misunderstanding, can wound you deeply. While you are infatuated, you have a glimpse of the unity that is possible, but you now feel cast out from Home. However, infatuation includes more than the play of love between a man and a woman. The feeling of ecstasy that you experience during a love relationship points toward a coming Home in the deeper sense of the word: to feel connected with the whole. You can experience this feeling intensely in a love relationship, and you can also feel it in other relationships, such as with a child, a friend, a pet, and in nature.

How can you preserve this sense of unity in your relationship as husband and wife? Is this possible in everyday life? How do you deal with the fear and misunderstanding that can arise between you and your spouse? The answer lies within you. Go within and find the open space in your heart from which you can connect without judgement with your own pain *and* that of the other. Become aware of old ideas that you cherish about how you as a man or a woman are supposed to be. The most important thing is to recognize your *own* pain and to become aware of your *own* blind spots. Then it becomes easier to have understanding for the fear and pain in the other. In this way, you build a bridge toward the other. In the open and honest acceptance of yourself, you create that bridge. The pain then does not cause you to contract and withdraw, *the pain then connects.*

## Pain as a bridge

When you say "Yes" to your own pain and do not flee from it – when you dare to descend into your own grief – you become yielding and at ease inside. You become gentle with yourself and that gentleness is also a bridge to the other. The other can be there also, with his or her own pain and inability to communicate and understand you. If you are gentle with yourself, and embrace your own dark places with open acceptance, you can forgive the other more easily and leave room for him or her to develop at their own pace. Simply put, there are two possibilities. Either you can allow the pain to stand between you and your loved one, like a wedge that pushes you further apart, or you can make it a bridge that connects you. This you do by sharing the pain, and without seeking solutions.

However, the sharing of pain is not the main thing. The crucial step lies in the openness and kindness toward each other. Through this step, you transcend your role as husband and wife, and your partnership is lifted to the level of the soul. You touch each other as *souls*, and at this level you know each other as equals. If there is true understanding and openness between two persons, both are lifted to the level of the soul.

So much love and inspiration can exist at the level of the soul that it radiates gently throughout your daily life and you both feel carried by joy and confidence. Through your connection with each other, your life gets a radiance that changes everything, yet you are still separate persons. Each of you still carries within you your own history, and each of you goes your own way and will again encounter shadow areas and blind spots within. It requires commitment and dedication from both of you to create a bridge to each other and to maintain the building of that bridge – *again and again.* You will be challenged constantly to let go of judgments and to open yourself to meet the other person. The bridge that makes it possible to meet each other at a soul level is built by your earthly hands.

In this time, many men and women feel the desire for a relationship that lifts them to the level of the soul. There is a sincerity in your desire that ensures that you naturally attract the right encounters in your life. *Let life surprise you!* Do not be guided by preconceived biases or expectations. Be prepared to build bridges, but start with yourself and observe how the other person touches you, encourages you, and challenges you. So many beautiful things can arise when people – men and women – are willing to meet one another in openness. The bridges you build in yourself are roads to a new future. Would it not be marvelous to live in a world where men and women are once again dancing together in wonder and respect for one another? What you create in yourself and in your relationship with another is the blueprint for the future. The key lies in your hands.

## Children of the new Earth

I would like to take you to the future. The future does not exist yet on a physical level, so it is not perceptible to your physical senses. However, seeds have been sown already, waiting for the right conditions to thrive. The future, in the present, is as an open, planted field full of potential, although nothing is for certain. We all know how much effort it takes to help a tender seed germinate and mature. Whether or not this field will flourish and grow into a garden of beauty and abundance lies partly in your hands.

You are the creators of the future on Earth. Do you create from trust and love, or do you act from fear and caution? To which seeds do you give the most nurturance and attention? In this message, I want to tell you what I consider to be the most promising seeds of the future. This time in which you live is distinguished by a number of possibilities and promises – a number of seeds which can bear rich fruits. I would like to discuss four: the promise of a shared humanity, the promise of an open heart, the promise of the new generation, and the promise of you.

## Shared humanity

There is, at this time more than ever before, the possibility of global communication on Earth. Through newspapers and magazines, radio and television and the internet, people are able to become acquainted with the lifestyle, stories, and emotions of people on the other side of the world. This offers the hope for a new perspective, for an ever greater awareness of what connects you as people: the pain, sorrow, and disillusion, and also the joy, courage, and hope. Now, more than ever before, you can see these emotions mirrored in the faces of others, and you can also recognize yourself in them. The other person may have a different color skin, have grown up in a different culture, speak a different language, and have different beliefs, yet there is a shared humanity.

This shared aspect of humanity is precisely what is becoming more visible through the free flow of information in the world. This movement toward exchange at a global level is good and natural. Only when people recognize one another as equals can there emerge a deep connection and cooperation. This felt tendency can build toward unification, and although there are still many obstacles on the path, there is already discussion of development toward a worldwide shared humanity.

## The opened heart

There are also more and more people on Earth who realize that material wealth, power, and success offer no lasting happiness and joy, and they are searching for another way of life. They desire a way of life that connects them with other people and with the planet on which they live, and this is an important step forward for humanity. As long as you are possessed with the desire to be successful, rich, or powerful, you live for yourself. I do not condemn this, because this lifestyle is often not born from a deliberate choice; rather it stems from fear, uncertainty, and a sense of lack.

In your deepest essence, you as human beings are not egocentric and power hungry. Deep within each of you is a longing for peace and emotional closeness with others, and being focused on success, wealth, or power is not a natural tendency. It arises from a sense of being rootless and ineffectual, and this is a sad way of being. In the past century, many people have experienced this condition within themselves, and some have actually acquired much success and wealth only to discover that there remained a void in their hearts. Many others have not acquired success and wealth, and they have experienced the hardness of a human society that defines you in terms of what you can do and what you have, instead of who you are in your true nature.

On whichever side you find yourself, and whether or not you can keep up with the "rat race", the fact is that now, for many people, there is the pain they experience through being separated from their true nature. It is because of this increasing pain that the realization is growing that to be focused *only* on performance, material prosperity, and success is a dead-end. More and more people desire to live from their hearts, and this desire carries a promise. When more and more people have a desire for a new way of living, the vision of a heart based society will begin to come alive in their dreams and plans for the future. Even though you do not know how your dreams and ideals will eventually manifest, it is the inner change in your heart that precedes the outer change and makes it possible. In many hearts, there is now a turnabout, and this change of direction becomes stronger when you believe in yourself and in the power of your heart-felt desires.

## The power of the new generation

The promises of a shared humanity and an open heart are increasingly realized by the new generation of children growing up today. Many children are now born with an open and sensitive heart. However, if you were born in, or before the 1960's, you grew up within a system of values that was still largely based on fear, coercion, and authority. You had to adapt to those values in order to survive and belong. Later in your life, you began to realize that as a result of this adaptation, something essential within you was lost. Through outer pressures, your inner voice and your original feelings became veiled, and sometimes it takes a crisis to make you aware that you want to rediscover what was lost, and that you want to come Home again to yourself.

The children who were born after the 1960s were brought up with less fear and coercion. This is a great achievement that has made life lighter on Earth. Parents who let their child grow up in openness, and who rely on the inner strength of the child, create a new educational ideal. Within this ideal, it is not so much the intention that the child adapt to existing values, rather it is the knowledge that the child has the innate ability to be open to receive the new. Every child carries the spark of the new within itself. Children naturally point out your lack of understanding and ingrained prejudices, and for this reason, the fact that children are different often calls up resentment and censure within the older generation. These children differ from what you are accustomed and from what you consider good and correct. In a spiritually mature society, the otherness and the new that children bring is seen as special: as a driving force for growth and development.

What is new about what today's children bring? They bring light, originality, and creativity, and they live more from their feelings, and what is decisive for them is what feels right and not what should or ought to be. They have fewer doubts about themselves and are less susceptible to coercion and discipline, although in another respect they are very sensitive. Through their open hearts, they easily respond to the pain of others. In their connection with others, there are fewer buffers, which makes them more vulnerable. This capability of responding too strongly to external stimuli, and the impressions and moods of others, can injure them. Even so, the children of today are helped by a powerful and conscious connection with nature: their own inner nature and the nature outside them. This can bring them back to their essence: who they actually are and what they have to give

Children who suffer from hypersensitivity, and therefore exhibit abnormal behavior, can no longer be brought to "normal" behavior by coercion and discipline. The lack of boundaries that such children exhibit in their behavior can be brought on track only by encouraging them to remain close to themselves and to keep both feet on the ground. They benefit from peace, simplicity, and grounding. This provides a counterbalance to their openness, sensitivity, and idealism.

The road to the New Earth must be presented to these children as something that is joyful and enriching. The only limits that today's children accept, are limits that come from within, from their hearts. Limits that are imposed from outside, from duty or morality, are experienced as a loss of self. Children of today will fight these limits "tooth and nail", although they do not do this simply from resistance or deliberate rebellion. Their response is a part of the spiritual message that this new generation of children is bringing to us, and the message and promise of these children is *freedom*: freedom from external coercion, from fear, and from authority; freedom to live from your own nature and to connect from there with the world around you.

You can promote this freedom by allowing yourself to follow the voice of *your* heart. This also allows you to "lighten up" as a person, and to be a beacon of light for the children who come after you. Whether you are young or old, you are a child of the New Earth that now, through you, wants to be born.

# The promise of you

This brings me to the last promise I want to discuss – the promise of *you*. This collection of messages is my call to you. I want to open your heart to the promise that lies within you: *the promise of a wonderful, free, and happy human being.* I love you *as you are*, and I want to make you aware of what you are and that you can become even more. I encourage you to embrace the life within yourself: the feelings, doubts, fears, and also the hope, the inspiration, and the joy. All this belongs to you and makes you human. The promise of who you are becoming will not be realized by you becoming a "better" human being but by you fully understanding and embracing who you are. Herein lies your greatest promise: *that you lovingly accept yourself as you are and embrace your own nature.* Let there be peace with who you are – with your pain and grief, with your hopes and desires – by surrendering your self to your *own* humanity and to your *own* nature.

Life wants to flow through you and to not be arranged and regulated, but to be *lived.* Life is there to be experienced, with all its highs and lows. It is in surrendering to the flow of life wherein lies your liberation. *Conscious surrender to life is the most powerful tool at your disposal.* In the letting go of your opposition to what is, an open space is created in your heart. Since there is no more judgment and expectation, life can flow through you freely. *You bend with the winds of life by swaying to the rhythm of your own nature.* This resilience allows you to experience a joy that does not depend on positive *or* negative experiences. This joy is independent of them both, and it occurs when you surrender to yourself – it occurs when you *live!*

I see who you are. I see your beauty and light even when you are immersed in doubt, fear and dark thoughts. I am your mother, and a mother sees the light in her children even if they themselves can not see it. Through the clouds, a mother sees the radiant sun that is always present. I would remind you of the sun that you are. Look at me, at the nature around you. Behold the light that radiates from the open air, from the natural flow of water, from a delicate flower – this light is also alive in *you.* We are one – see yourself mirrored in the beauty of the Earth. Hear and see my call to you.

## *Other books by Pamela Kribbe*

### The Jeshua Channelings

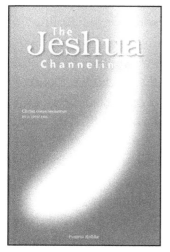

In clear and accessible language, Jeshua speaks about the origins and destiny of the lightworker family. He offers a detailed account of the transition from ego-based to heart-based consciousness. In the second part of the book, Jeshua deals with several aspects of everyday life, such as relationships, work and health. He addresses the most common questions and problems we struggle with in these areas.

*Some books are filled with shining wisdom. Others radiate great love. A few – a very rare few – are overflowing with both. The Jeshua Channelings is one such book. If you want to know who you really are, why you're here, and what your life is truly about, look no further. This book gently and compassionately guides readers toward remembering their magnificence as divine souls. Brilliantly insightful and inspiring, it is true gem and a blessing to our world.*

- Robert Schwartz, author, Your Soul's Plan: Discovering the Real Meaning of the Life You Planned Before You Were Born - yoursoulsplan.com

**ISBN-13:** 978-1601456823
**Paperback:** 264 pages
**Publisher:** Booklocker.com, Inc.

## Heart Centered Living

Heart Centered Living is living according to the calling of your soul. You can recognize the calling of your soul by the feelings of joy, peace and inspiration it brings to you. However, daring to trust your heart often involves a leap into the unknown. You may be confronted with deep-seated fears about your own worth and your ability to pursue your own path. This book is a loving guide on your way to heart centered living. It contains clear and informative channelings inspired by the Christ energy. They deal with different subjects, such as finding your true passion, how to create balanced relationships, parenting the new, sensitive children and emotional healing in the face of fear and depression. They also speak about the profound transformation humanity is going through, letting go of ego-based consciousness and evolving into heart-based consciousness.

This book is written for lightworkers, souls who feel compelled to go deep within and express their true soul's calling on Earth. The teachers who speak in this book (Jeshua, Mary and mother Earth) all encourage you to take the leap of faith and become who you really are. Their teachings gently inspire you to face and overcome whatever holds you back in listening to the voice of your heart.

**ISBN-13:** 978-1621412618
**Paperback:** 276 pages
**Publisher:** Booklocker.com, Inc.

## The Christ Within

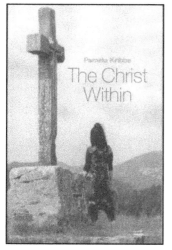

In each of us, Christ consciousness is waiting to be awakened. Christ consciousness is the awareness that behind outer appearance and form, all life is one and connected. As we enter this level of awareness, we gradually let go of our fear, our resistance, our need to control. We discover the reality of our divine essence, our soul. Life becomes less about struggling to survive, driven by the demands of the ego, and more about joy and creating from the heart.

Opening up to the voice of our soul involves taking a leap into the abyss: you are invited to rely on your inner guidance rather than the outer directions you are used to steering by. How do you let go of the worldly pressures and judgments that have become almost second nature? How do you know if you have truly connected with your soul? How do you deal with fear and trauma, which keeps you from surrendering?

The spiritual messages in this book, received by way of channeling, are meant to answer these questions and to assist you on your path of inner transformation in a loving and compassionate way. As you surrender to your soul, the Christ Within will awaken and illuminate your life as well as the lives of others.

**ISBN-13**: 978-1626469631
**Paperback**: 264 pages
**Publisher**: Booklocker.com, Inc.

## Dark Night of the Soul

This book contains Pamela's personal story of the deepest crisis she ever experienced in her life. Successful as a writer and spiritual therapist, she was confronted first with illness, then with insomnia and fear, and ultimately with depression and psychosis. She had to be hospitalized and undergo psychiatric treatment. Pamela openly describes what she went through and also seeks to come to terms with what happened to her from a spiritual perspective. What do depression and psychosis mean from the perspective of the soul? How do they arise and can they bear fruit? What is the role of psychiatry in a dark night of the soul?

The second part of the book contains a series of channeled messages about the meaning of severe crises in our lives, the need to face our own darkness, and the unfailing presence of love and compassion in our lives.

**ISBN-13:** 978-1634908788
**Paperback:** 248 pages
**Publisher:** Booklocker.com, Inc.

## The Forbidden Female Speaks

Mary Magdalene was regarded as "the forbidden female" in the Christian tradition: wild, free and sinful. This book contains a dialogue with and messages from Mary Magdalene, channeled by Pamela Kribbe (PhD). It is about male and female energy, relationships, sexuality and healing. In these teachings, Mary Magdalene speaks with a clear, loving voice that is sometimes direct and confrontational but mostly compassionate and deeply appreciative of human nature.

In both men and women, there is a forbidden female energy, Mary Magdalene says, which has to do with feeling, intuition and the heart. In this day and age, both sexes are invited to become aware of this energy and to heal the old wound of separation between them. In this way, we will learn how to listen to our heart's whispers again and reconnect with our soul.

**ISBN-13:** 978-1632637048
**Paperback:** 200 pages
**Publisher:** Booklocker.com, Inc.

## Acknowledgements

My gratitude goes to Gerrit Gielen with whom I have an unconditional soul connection that has been a source of inspiration and support in writing this book.

I appreciate the presence and trust of all the people who attended the workshops from which the channelings in the second part of this book arose.

I am grateful to Maria Baes for translating this book from Dutch into English with skill and passion. Thank you to Frank Tehan for his invaluable editing work.

## *Contact details*

www.jeshua.net

info@jeshua.net

CPSIA information can be obtained
at www.ICGtesting.com
Printed in the USA
BVHW030952060521
606651BV00004B/82